MW01051429

THE EXCHANGE

*Journey from
Hurting to Hope*

COPYRIGHT

The Exchange: Journey from Hurting to Hope by Karrie Garcia

Published by Freedom Movement | Orange, CA

www.wearefreedommovement.org

© 2018 Karrie Garcia

www.karriegarcia.com

ISBN: 978-1-7323561-0-8

All rights reserved. No portion of this book may be reproduced, stored or transmitted in any form for example electronic, photocopy or recording - without prior written permission from the publisher, except as permitted by U.S. copyright law. The only exception is brief quotations in printed reviews. For permissions contact: hello@wearefreedommovement.org. Please encourage and participate in doing the right thing.

Scripture quotations marked NIV are taken from the Holy Bible, NEW INTERNATIONAL VERSION®, NIV® Copyright © 1973, 1978, 1984, 2011 by Biblica, Inc.® Used by permission. All rights reserved worldwide. Scripture quotations marked NLT are taken from the Holy Bible, New Living Translation, copyright © 1996, 2004, 2015 by Tyndale House Foundation. Used by permission of Tyndale House Publishers, Inc., Carol Stream, Illinois 60188. All rights reserved. Scripture quotations marked MSG are taken from The Message. Copyright © 1993, 1994, 1995, 1996, 2000, 2001, 2002. Used by permission of NavPress Publishing Group. Scripture quotations marked ESV are taken from the ESV® Bible (The Holy Bible, English Standard Version®), copyright © 2001 by Crossway, a publishing ministry of Good News Publishers. Used by permission. All rights reserved. Scripture quotations marked NASB are taken from the New American Standard Bible® (NASB), Copyright © 1960, 1962, 1963, 1968, 1971, 1972, 1973, 1975, 1977, 1995 by The Lockman Foundation Used by permission. www.Lockman.org. Scripture Quotations marked NKJV are taken from the New King James Version®. Copyright © 1982 by Thomas Nelson. Used by permission. All rights reserved.

This work is sold with the understanding that neither the author nor the publisher are held responsible for the results attained from following the advice in this book. We highly recommend seeking professional care if needed.

Cover design by Makenzie Riley, www.makenzieriley.com
Book design and production by Mario Garcia & Makenzie Riley
Content editing by Melanie Vogel
Copy editing by Sara Grexton & Juliana Hilmerson
Author photograph by Michelle Sullivan

DEDICATION

/

THIS BOOK IS DEDICATED TO MY MOTHER, LINDA SCOTT. SHE HAD A DEEP DESIRE TO SHARE THE TRUTH OF GOD'S LOVE, BUT NEVER FELT QUALIFIED TO DO SO. BECAUSE OF THIS, IT'S MY HEART TO BE THE VOICE OF HOPE, TRUTH AND LOVE SHE COULDN'T BE. IT'S MY PRAYER, AND I BELIEVE IT WOULD ALSO BE MY MOM'S, THAT EVERY WOMAN WOULD KNOW SHE IS NOT ALONE AND THAT THERE IS A TRIBE FOR HER.

THIS BOOK ALSO IS DEDICATED TO THE MANY WOMEN WHO ARE HURTING, DESPERATE, AND LOOKING FOR ANSWERS. I LOVE YOU. YOU ARE SEEN. MY PRAYER IS THAT YOU WILL EXPERIENCE THE RADICAL LOVE OF GOD AND THAT IT BRINGS THE HOPE FOR WHICH YOU HAVE BEEN LONGING.

ACKNOWLEDGEMENTS

TIM SCOTT
Without your reckless, pursuant love for me, I never would have started to understand how deeply God loves me. Your teachings and grace are all over every single page of this book. You are my hero and the closest example of how vast God's love is for me. I love you more than words will ever express.

MELANIE VOGEL
For your tireless editing, attention to detail, and SOLID belief in this project.

KIMBERLY SCOTT
For being a mom to this wounded girl and my biggest fan. You healed places in my heart I never knew could be healed.

RYDER, ROCCO, AND ROMA
You are my redemption and the best things I have ever created. You made every word in this book real, and I am a better person because of you three. Mommy loves you.

FREEDOM MOVEMENT TEAM
For believing in me when I didn't even believe in myself. You show me daily that freedom is possible, that love is beautiful, and that women are amazing!

JULIANA HILMERSON
For executing every crazy thought and believing in the dreams and visions in my wandering brain. You are my peace.

MICHELLE SULLIVAN
For being loyal since the beginning, and for having a faith that makes my faith bigger.

MARIO GARCIA
You are my safest place. I could never do what I do without you by my side. You are more than my husband, or my friend, or my confidant. You are the one. I am so proud to be your wife. Thank you for loving others with such a big heart and for taking on this calling for our family. I respect you more than anyone in this world. I will forever be honored to be by your side.

HOW TO USE THIS BOOK
*SUITABLE FOR INDIVIDUAL OR GROUP USE.

01   **BE OPEN** to whatever the Holy Spirit is wanting to reveal to you during this time. God is interested in intimacy with you and freedom for you, so commit to being open and all in.

02   **WEEK ONE:**

/ **Read the introduction on page 8 first.** You'll learn why I wrote this course and why it's been my life's call to do so.

/ **Access the videos via wearefreedommovement.org/exchangevideos + watch the introduction video.** This will get you (and your group, if applicable) started on the journey.

/ **Answer the introduction questions.** These questions help prepare your heart for what God has for you in the weeks ahead.

/ **Discuss your answers.** If you're working through this course with a group or friend, share with one another. If you're doing it individually, share with God.

/ **Watch the "Reckless Love" video, then follow the process below.**

03   **EACH FOLLOWING WEEK:**

/ **Start each week by watching the accompanying video.**
If you are working in a group, spend 30-60 minutes sharing your answers to the prior week's "Weekly Big 3" questions. Then, watch the current week's video.

/ **Do your homework.** Dedicate time in your week to work through this workbook uninterrupted. Complete every exercise and journal reflection — they were designed to solidify what you learn.

/ **Answer the "Weekly Big 3" and prepare to reflect on your answers next week.**

04   **SHARE YOUR JOURNEY:**

/ Share your reflections, your discoveries, and your questions on social media by using **#theexchangecourse**.

TOOLS YOU WILL NEED:

BIBLE

JOURNAL

PEN OR PENCIL

STICKY NOTES

It's brave for someone to share something they're struggling with

FOR GROUP LEADERS

· Create a safe place

· Thank you for sharing
· Reminder to keep it a safe place

· don't try to fix.

· Thank them for being there.

01 **Organize group meeting place and time.** Encourage full participation and establish confidentiality to create a safe place for sharing.

02 **Make sure everyone has their own book.** Due to the personal nature of the exercises, sharing workbooks is discouraged.

03 **Remind your group that they will be discussing their "Weekly Big 3" at the beginning of each meeting. Encourage them to come prepared to share.**

04 **Create a comfortable, welcoming, and relaxed atmosphere.** Snacks, coffee, and water are always a good idea.

05 **Your main job is to facilitate group questions, but do not feel the need to have all the answers.** Holy Spirit will do a great job of revealing where a person needs to be.

06 **Allow two hours for each meeting.** As the leader, be respectful of time by starting and ending on time. This is vital.

07 **Good leaders are honest and real.** Be prepared to share your experience throughout the journey, and let your group know you are one of them. This will bring about a "me, too" atmosphere and will encourage vulnerability.

08 **On the last week, watch the closing video and discuss the final "Weekly Big 3" and course reflection.** I find it helpful to allow space for sharing overall reflections, and then end in prayer. Remind all ladies that it's normal if sections of the process have brought up feelings that need to be explored in more depth. Encourage them to dive deeper into those areas with a mentor, counselor, or maybe more readings on the particular topic.

09 **Give HUGS!** Let them know how proud you are of them and how much you respect them for pursuing freedom!

HEY FRIENDS!

I am so proud of you for caring about your freedom! I wrote this course based on the path I walked to experience freedom in my life. I learned what it means to exchange my hurts for God's healing, and that has radically changed my life. As you begin (or continue) this journey, you likely will face obstacles, difficult moments, or pain that will make you want to stop. Please hang in there – your freedom is worth it! Though exchanging an old idea or hurt can make you feel exposed and scared, I encourage you to fight past the fear and continue to pursue the abundant life God has for you.

Don't fear freedom, friends! You are worth fighting for. The good news is God is a good Father who is gentle and kind. He knows the fragile places of your heart that feel wounded and He wants to free you from that pain. You are not alone in this journey. I stand with you and am cheering you on from the sidelines. As you go through this course, I encourage you to share with a trusted friend or go through it with a group. It is so encouraging when you know you are not alone. Processing out loud what you are going through is therapeutic and helps the healing process.

This course is in no way intended to take place of the written Word of God, which is the true source of all your healing. I have done my best to use God's Word to teach you some tools for getting on the other side of hurt. There may be a section that stops you in your tracks. Make a note of this and return to this section once you've completed the course to explore what God is revealing.

DON'T FEAR FREEDOM, FRIENDS! YOU ARE WORTH FIGHTING FOR.

This book is a guide that I still use and refer to ALL THE TIME. Do not feel disheartened if you are not magically better at the end of the nine weeks. You will be farther than when you started, you will know more about God's love for you, and you will be more aware of areas in your life that are longing for freedom. This is more than most people will know in a lifetime, so you'll be doing great!

I have prayed over each page, I have walked through the steps myself, and I have personally seen hundreds of women walk in more victory when they apply the truths of this course to their lives. I know that God has so much to reveal to you, so be open and commit — you're worth it!

Over the next nine weeks, put yourself first, go all in, and watch as God moves you from hurting to hope.

Hope is Here,

INTRO
BIG 3

01   What are you hoping to gain from taking this course?

What fears do you have about going through this journey?   **02**

03   What benefits would come from you being ALL IN? What does "all in" mean to you?

01. LOVE

"BUT GOD, BEING RICH IN MERCY, BECAUSE OF THE GREAT
LOVE WITH WHICH HE LOVED US, EVEN WHEN WE WERE
DEAD IN OUR TRESPASSES, MADE US ALIVE TOGETHER
WITH CHRIST- BY GRACE YOU HAVE BEEN SAVED."
EPHESIANS 2:4-5

VIDEO NOTES

01. LOVE

When I set out to create this course, I was so tempted to jump straight into the healing process. I wanted to throw you into the proverbial deep waters of pursuing freedom in your life – because God wants you free! However, through prayer, Jesus took me back to the dark, healing days of my journey and to the first moment I knew I needed help. In those moments, I realized, God pursued and loved me recklessly – and that is the foundation of healing.

As the movie reel of my life played in my mind, I began to notice God's ever-present love in my life. Far before my life hit rock bottom, He was calling me, powerfully speaking to me OVER AND OVER again. Relentlessly, He pursued me with one thing I could never escape: LOVE. So, before we take any steps in this healing process, it is imperative that you first understand how much God loves you. You must learn to recognize the presence of His love in your life, and then allow it to become your new identity.

As you heard me share about the story of Hosea and Gomer, you saw that what was asked of Hosea was nothing short of CRAZY! I mean, to go after his wife after she had GONE BACK to a life of prostitution? Surely God was asking too much!

Through Hosea's love for Gomer, God ultimately shows us the way He loves us. No matter how many times we turn our backs on Him, He searches for us, He paid for us with His Son, and He reconciles us back to Him! Here is what I have come to understand about the love of GOD – it is radical!

God knew that in order for us to have access to His relentless love there must be an exchange – the ultimate exchange when God chose to offer His Son for our freedom. We are so undeserving of this kind of sacrifice, but God did not want heaven without us in it! This exchange is what we are always trying to get back to – our sin for His righteousness, our pain for His freedom, and our deserved destiny for His purposed plan.

Until we can FULLY understand the sacrifice and the LOVE it must have taken to allow His own Son to die on our behalf, we will never understand the fullness of our freedom. So, my hope is that you come back to the cross every day to rest in the place where everything you have ever done or has been done to you was nailed and taken.

> *But He was pierced for our transgressions, He was crushed for our iniquities; the punishment that brought us peace was on Him, and by His wounds we are healed.*
> *Isaiah 53:5 (NIV)*
>
> **WHAT DOES THIS VERSE MEAN TO YOU TODAY?**

JOURNAL REFLECTION

Have you allowed yourself to receive the gift of God's love? Take a few minutes to pray. Let your Father know that you no longer want to live without His covering over you. Pray to receive this FREE gift from God. There is no magic way to do this; it is just expressing to your Father that you are tired of doing life on your own and you want Him to be Lord over your life and heart. If you have already stepped into a relationship with God, pray a prayer of thankfulness.

If we remember the incredible exchange made for our lives every day, we will live in more peace and courage.

In fact, if we remember the great exchange, then no matter what happens, this will always be enough!

Write this prayer of thankfulness in your journal.

RECOGNIZING GOD'S LOVE IN MY LIFE

During my darkest times, there were many moments when I didn't believe God loved me. I knew I didn't deserve His love, so I rejected it. But, no matter what, there it was. He showed me His love through my imperfect parents and He showed me in the quiet nights of my shame and guilt. From when I opened my eyes in the morning until I went to sleep: love. When I would reluctantly go to church and even when I wanted to end it all: LOVE.

I never really thought about it until I took a step back and looked over my life. God's love was always comforting me and begging me to come to HIM. People judged me and wrote me off. My parents were hurt and broken and I often viewed His love for me through that grid. I thought He loved the way others loved. I WAS WRONG. He loved me in my darkest moments and, finally, after years of fighting and hopelessness, I decided to see if He really meant it.

Turning from my broken behavior, going to therapy, digging into *why* I was hurting, forgiving all those who had wronged me, and forgiving myself for those I had wronged were all part of the journey of healing. BUT, I want to make something crystal clear: NONE of my healing could have happened if it were not for God's love for me.

Why did I fight against this gift for so long? Why didn't I cry out to Him sooner? The hurt that I felt, the things I had done, and the things that had happened to me caused me to believe that I was not worth this kind of love. I thought, "I better get it together, and when I do, only then will I be worthy of this kind of love." Boy, was I wrong. I wasted so many years believing God was like humans: judgmental and harsh. I believed He had boxes for me to check, and, until I checked them all, I couldn't be close to Him. Again, I was so wrong.

Jeremiah 31:3 declares that He loves us "with an everlasting love." EVERLASTING. This means it never ends! His love has no stipulations and is simply waiting to be received.

I am so thankful for all the tools I learned to get the help I needed, but none of those tools would have mattered if I didn't know how deeply I am loved. I would have been trying in my own power to "fix me." That may have worked for a while, but nothing heals the deepest parts of your soul like the pure love of God.

Something happens to us when we realize we are loved — especially when we know we don't deserve it. Love heals in ways nothing else can, and without it, we have nothing. When I realized God truly loves me, I was able to see myself through that grid. It was a challenge because my self-destructive brain wanted to revert to shame and judgment, but God's love would not let me. It surrounded me. His love gave me a new identity, hope, and purpose.

Over time, Christ's pure love changed my name from "Defeated" to "Overcomer." I AM LOVED and not only am I loved, I am HIS! ME! The girl who has made mistake after mistake, who was abandoned, and who brought shame upon her family and herself: SHE IS LOVED. How can this be? It's because God does not love with human love. His love is perfect and untainted by human junk. When I felt like giving up, HIS love would scream to me, "YOU ARE MINE! Don't believe the lies! Trust Me and I WILL SET YOU FREE!"

WHAT HAVE YOU BELIEVED ABOUT
GOD'S LOVE IN THE PAST?

HOW HAS THAT AFFECTED
YOUR PRESENT LIFE?

His love gives us a new identity, hope, and purpose.

RECOGNIZING THE POWER OF GOD'S PURE LOVE

By realizing the power of this love and beginning to trust that what Jesus said is true, then, and only then, will your heart start to change. His love gives you a new identity. It causes you to be identified by something new, and by Someone perfect. Instead of being identified by your pain, you are identified by the King of Kings and Creator of the Universe. You are His most beloved – and that changes everything!

This doesn't mean the struggle is gone, but you now know that you are not alone. His love gives you courage to fight for healing. During my healing, I remember thinking that the fight to be healed was more than I could bear. As I would cry out to God, He would love on me. He would give me the courage to keep going, telling me that healing was coming. It was His love for me that ministered to me. When you are identified by God's love, you are given a new name. A new identity starts to rise up within your soul and the things that controlled you before no longer have power.

We often believe that there are certain things we have done or things that have been done to us that cannot be healed. We believe that our wounds go too deep. These are lies, sister! NOTHING can separate us from the love of God. In order to truly be a conqueror, you must believe this truth. Memorize this and place it on your heart. All of these truths about God's love must be the fabric of how you identify yourself. God's love never leaves you, it sees beyond all your pain and mistakes, and it causes you to rise above everything that has happened.

"
NOTHING CAN SEPARATE US FROM THE LOVE OF GOD.

Let's start to place the truth of who you are into your mind and heart. It is so important to know who you truly are. God has a new name for you. He wants to change the lies you tell yourself — even if you don't realize they are lies. We live a victorious life when our identity is placed in our true selves. When our pain is our identity, we can never get past that pain. God's Word says that you are HIS CHILD. That means you are an heir to His throne, you wear a crown upon your head, and He holds you in a place of honor. NO MATTER WHERE YOU ARE, you are His child. Let this become your true identity!

GOD'S LOVE SEEN IN SCRIPTURE

As you heard in the video, Gomer was offered a new life in exchange for her old one. She knew Hosea loved her, but she never felt worthy enough to receive it. It wasn't until Hosea humiliated himself, bought her back, and took her into his home once again that she knew the depth of his love.

When God gave up His Son for you, it was for your freedom — so your old life passes away and you receive a NEW life in Him!

NIV /

Therefore, if anyone is in Christ, the new creation has come: The old has gone, the new is here! All this is from God, who reconciled us to Himself through Christ and gave us the ministry of reconciliation: that God was reconciling the world to Himself in Christ, not counting people's sins against them. And He has committed to us the message of reconciliation.
2 Corinthians 5:17-19

Many of us have read this scripture often, but we rarely tap into the power of claiming this truth! Whenever you start to feel the demons of your past resurface, or you feel your present circumstances are insurmountable, you havethe power to claim this truth in that moment! I AM NEW. I don't have to be defined by anything other than the cross, where Jesus' life was sacrificed to make me new.

EXERCISE
Understanding God's Love

Take a couple minutes to reflect on what you just read. Then, answer these questions:

Think back on your past. Whether you noticed it at the time or not, when has God shown you His love? What was your response?

What is keeping you from accepting this gift of love?

How would your life change if you could fully accept God's love for you?

To understand what God's Word says about His love, read these verses and write down what God is revealing to you.

EPHESIANS 2:4-5

ROMANS 5:8

PSALM 86:15

JOHN 10:10

Read the following passage, and then answer the questions below.

> *Who shall separate us from the love of Christ? Shall tribulation, or distress, or persecution, or famine, or nakedness, or danger, or sword? As it is written, "For Your sake we are being killed all the day long; we are regarded as sheep to be slaughtered." No, in all these things we are more than conquerors through Him who loved us. For I am sure that neither death nor life, nor angels nor rulers, nor things present nor things to come, nor powers, nor height nor depth, nor anything else in all creation, will be able to separate us from the love of God in Christ Jesus our Lord.* **Romans 8:35-39 (ESV)**
>
> **WHAT CAN SEPARATE US FROM GOD'S LOVE?**

> **BASED ON THIS PASSAGE, WHAT SPECIFIC THINGS IN YOUR OWN LIFE DOES GOD'S LOVE NEED TO CONQUER?**

JOURNAL REFLECTION

Spend some time writing what part of your old life needs to be exchanged for new. That might be your hurts, your worries, or anything that keeps you stuck in the old way of thinking. I find that when we acknowledge the truth of how loved we are, the awesome sacrifice that has been made on our behalf, and the new life that we are offered, we gain a new perspective.

It's not enough to know

what God has done for us.

We must CLAIM IT!

When you find yourself drifting back into the old, STOP, claim His love for you, and never settle for your old identity. Invite God to come into that place where you are stuck and allow Him to begin to heal you. Invitation is key to this process; it allows Him to be Lord over that wounded area. Don't fear the freedom that comes when you allow Him to enter the broken places of your heart.

WEEKLY BIG 3

01
_____

What is God asking you to release to Him this week? What will you receive in exchange?

What "aha!" moments or chapter highlights stood out to you this week?
02
_____

03
_____

What three next steps can you take as you continue making exchanges with God?

02. IDENTITY

"FOR AS HE THINKS WITHIN HIMSELF, SO HE IS."
PROVERBS 23:7

VIDEO NOTES

02. IDENTITY

What comes to mind when you hear the word "victim?" Perhaps you think of someone who has been traumatized. It may bring thoughts of rape, abuse, molestation, or other severe offenses. Yes, those who have suffered these things truly are victims. I want to challenge you, however, to think beyond the circumstances you think cause victimhood, as well as the kinds of people you most often consider victims.

I also want to challenge you with this question: *Do you consider yourself a victim?* I know it's a tough realization, but the first step on the road to victory is identifying if you view yourself as a victim.

IDENTIFYING A VICTIM MENTALITY

If you look up "victim" in a dictionary, you'll get a definition like this: ***"A victim is a person who is deceived or cheated, as by his or her own emotions or ignorance, by the dishonesty of others, or by some impersonal agency."*** Is this how you view yourself?

If we really stop and think about it, I believe most of us can say we've been hurt or wronged by someone at some point in our lives. Though this is true, the true risk is in allowing your victimhood or your pain to become your identity. When we do this, we live with a victim mentality and allow pain and shame to define who we are.

To discover if you have a victim mentality, ask yourself, "Am I stuck thinking about the wrongs that I have done or that have been done to me?" If your answer is yes, or if you struggle with anger, anxiety, depression, or guilt, or if you're consumed with shame, you may have a victim mentality. If in your mind your life has become the sum of your pain, you are living in a victim mentality. Essentially, if fear, worry, shame, or other deprecating emotions define your identity, you are living as a victim.

When you have a victim mentality, you see yourself through the grid of your pain. No matter what you do, deep within you, the pain of your past becomes the grid through which you see everything. When that grid is tainted with pain and shame, it is almost impossible to live in freedom.

For many, the hurts that have happened over the years have mentally taken a toll. The world tells us to "be tough; power through." In doing so, we never really deal with what hurts on the inside and we really never get to the bottom of why we are doing harmful things in our minds or to our bodies. If you're struggling with a victim mentality, you may feel the world is against you and that it's a place to fear. You may never feel you can break away from what you have done wrong or what was done to you. Peace, joy, and freedom may seem like foreign concepts to you.

Remember when Naomi only saw her life through the grid of her loss? Not only could she not see past her pain and circumstance, but she allowed it to change her name! She took on a name that identified her as her pain. As we read, we see her "live up to" the name she gave herself. Pushing away those who loved her, she became bitter and hopeless and felt as if there was no chance for her in life.

The truth is that victims live their lives believing lies about themselves. Does this sound like you? Whether you have had a treacherous act committed against you, or you were the one that committed the act, the lie is the same: you feel worthless and thoughts of anxiety, hopelessness, and rage fill your mind.

How can you start to break free from all this bondage? How do you change the grid through which you look at life? These are tough questions, but God has the answers and wants you to live the life He created for you.

EXERCISE
Where Is My Mind?

As we went over in this week's video, a victim mentality can occur when life meets loss. After filling in the diagrams on the next two pages, answer the following questions.

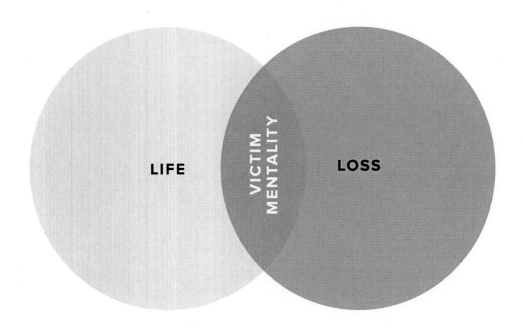

LIFE — VICTIM MENTALITY — LOSS

**What losses have you experienced
in your life?**

LOSS

Write some of the losses you have experienced.

HOW I SEE MYSELF

How have these experiences affected how you see yourself?

HOW I LIVE

How has this affected the way you live your life?

What are you trying to control that is out of your control?

Does fear or anxiety play a part in the way you make decisions? How?

What did you learn about yourself while filling out these diagrams?

How have your losses affected how you've lived your life?

"FOR I KNOW THE PLANS I HAVE FOR YOU," DECLARES THE LORD, "PLANS TO PROSPER YOU AND NOT TO HARM YOU, PLANS TO GIVE YOU HOPE AND A FUTURE."

JEREMIAH 29:11 (NIV)

BREAKING FREE FROM A VICTIM MENTALITY

GET HONEST

NASB /

We are destroying speculations and every lofty thing raised up against the knowledge of God, and we are taking every thought captive to the obedience of Christ.
2 Corinthians 10:5

To move towards freedom and victory, you must acknowledge the lies you are telling yourself – and lay them before the Lord. It's also important to recognize the sin or pain that is keeping you from Him. No more secrets!
You must get real to get healed.

For some, getting honest may be difficult. If you know that you are hurting, but can't really figure out why, or if you feel stuck, but don't know what's holding you back, ask God to search you. Psalm 139:23 reads "Search me, God, and know my heart; test me and know my anxious thoughts."

Pray that God helps you find the root of your pain. We can only move forward when we face our lies head on.

EXERCISE
Lies That Keep Me Stuck

If you're like me, your self talk may include lies like:

I'm worthless.
I'm stupid.
I'm a lost cause.
I'm ugly.
I'm disgusting.
I'm pathetic.
I'm a mistake.
I'm unwanted.
I'm undeserving.
I'm alone.
I'm a disappointment.
I'm disqualified.

What are the top three lies you tell yourself?

Can you remember a time you were free from these lies?

When did these lies begin to take root?

REPLACE LIES WITH TRUTH

NASB /

Finally, brethren, whatever is true, whatever is honorable, whatever is right, whatever is pure, whatever is lovely, whatever is of good repute, if there is any excellence and if anything worthy of praise, dwell on these things. The things you have learned and received and heard and seen in me, practice these things, and the God of peace will be with you.
Philippians 4:8-9

In order to move past these lies, we must replace them with the truth of who God says we are. When He says we are "no longer a slave" to our past sins (Romans 6:18), He really means it! However, it takes practice to reverse the tape we play in our minds. God's Word says to think on new things, good things, HOLY things. PRACTICE this!

Practice is the key to developing new habits; it's like learning to drive in a new way. I drove a stick shift for most of my life – up until a few years ago, in fact. (When I got my automatic car, I was so happy because, HELLO, I'm old now and I deserve to relax while I drive!) When I first got my new car, my left foot would reach for the clutch, causing a jerking motion in my body and the car. It was such a scene. My brain had "automatically" been doing this motion for so long that it took a while to retrain my brain to drive this new way.

The same is true for you. It takes practice to retrain the pathways in your brain to think new things. This won't happen overnight; it is a journey – but it can be done! I have seen women become new more times than I can count. The old ways of thinking do not define them anymore. They finally start to not only find new words to describe themselves, but they actually start *believing* that this is really their identity!

REDEFINING YOUR IDENTITY IN GOD

ESV

See what kind of love the Father has given to us, that we should be called children of God; and so we are. The reason why the world does not know us is that it did not know Him. Beloved, we are God's children now, and what we will be has not yet appeared; but we know that when He appears we shall be like Him, because we shall see Him as He is.
1 John 3:1-2

Who Does God Say You Are?

God says you are HIS CHILD. The Creator of the Universe says you are HIS, not just a distant relative or a congregational member at one of His churches. You are HIS CHILD. Let that sink in for a minute.

When you step into faith in Christ, whether or not your life has looked "good" does not change WHO you belong to or that you are identified by His greatness. The knowledge that our Heavenly Father takes ownership of us helps us realize we have all the power to walk in victory. We now are in the bloodline of the King of Kings!!! WHAT?! This blows my mind all the time. Jesus Christ not only calls you His, BUT He lives in you and so does His power. It's true that you may not be accessing that power right now, but YOU CAN!

> *"*
>
> # *NOT ONLY DOES GOD SAY YOU ARE HIS CHILD, BUT HE ALSO SAYS YOU ARE HOLY.*

OWNING YOUR IDENTITY AS GOD'S BELOVED

The first foundational step in changing who you are and the way you think is to know WHOSE you are – God's. If you always identify yourself with the pain you have caused or the pain that has been inflicted upon you, you will never move past it. However, when you begin to realize whose you are and the power that lives inside you, the bar is raised and you are no longer identified by your hurt, but rather by His name! Not only does God say you are His child, He also says you are HOLY! This did not come with a prerequisite of behavior change. This came with the knowledge that you are His daughter.

I am the daughter of Tim Scott. I have his looks, his characteristics, and even his sense of humor. I am very much my dad's daughter. When I was going through my years of drug addiction, this didn't change. Yes, I was not acting much like my father, or embracing who he had encouraged me to be, BUT I was still his. During the many years I walked away from his love – the years I embarrassed him and hurt him – I NEVER stopped being his daughter. In fact, not only was I his, but everything he had was mine, too. If something were to have happened to him, everything he had would have been mine – despite my actions. Everyone knows I am Tim Scott's daughter, and no matter what I do in life, that truth will never change.

This is how God sees you. Not only are you His, but you get all He has! He has chosen you (yes, you!) – the good, the bad, and the ugly. When He sees you, He identifies you by your true self, righteous and holy. In fact, He sees you as royal!

NASB /

But you are A CHOSEN RACE, A ROYAL PRIESTHOOD, A HOLY NATION, A PEOPLE FOR GOD'S OWN POSSESSION, so that you may proclaim the excellencies of Him who has called you out of darkness into His marvelous light; for you once were NOT A PEOPLE, but now you are THE PEOPLE OF GOD; you had NOT RECEIVED MERCY,
but now you have RECEIVED MERCY.
I Peter 2:9-10, Emphasis Added

JOURNAL REFLECTION

Look back on the times in your life when you found yourself functioning through the grid of a victim mentality. Write about the good that was in front of you that you may have missed because your focus was on what you didn't have or what was lost.

Take time to reflect upon the good.

This will help take back those hurtful moments and replace them with the good of what was around you during that time. This perspective shift will help start to free you from the pain of those memories.

EXERCISE
Proclaiming My True Identity

PART ONE:

It's time to start owning who you are; and assume your rightful place in the Kingdom of God. No more shame and no more hiding. Walking confidently in who you are in Christ and claiming how He sees you will begin the freeing work of changing the reel that plays over and over in your mind. This will redefine who you are!

When we walk with a victim mentality, we often miss the good that is right in front of us. Go back to the story in Ruth and read chapter one.

How different would Naomi's life have looked if she knew her true identity?

PART TWO:

There is power and healing in naming your true identity. Take some time to look up the passages below to discover some of those names. Then, write what you think God is revealing about who you are by beginning each response with "I AM."

ACTS 13:38
I AM...

JEREMIAH 31:3
I AM...

JOHN 1:12
I AM...

PSALM 139
I AM...

COLOSSIANS 1:13-14
I AM...

I PETER 2:9

I AM...

JOHN 16:33

I AM...

2 TIMOTHY 1:7

I AM...

MATTHEW 11:28-30

I AM...

Now, take a moment to look at the lies you wrote on page 43. Replacing these lies with the truth of who you truly are will open your mind to a new way of thinking. When you do this, you will start to believe you are who God says you are.

PART THREE:

Find a truth or two from God's Word that speaks to your heart. Write these truths down on sticky notes, it could be the whole Scripture or just a word from it that gives truth to your lie. Then, place them around your house, maybe on your bathroom mirror, in your car, or on your refrigerator. Essentially, place them anywhere you struggle to have good thoughts about yourself, or where you will see them often. God wants us to dwell on thoughts that bring life and freedom, not on the lies that rob or bind us.

Pray that the truth of these statements sink in and start to change the way you think. God cares deeply for you and it grieves Him to see you living in bondage and lies. When you pray, ask Him to come in and continue to reveal truth to you. You will be amazed at the different ways God is going to reveal His love for you!

**PLACE YOUR
FIRST STICKY
NOTE HERE!**

WEEKLY BIG 3

01 What is God asking you to release to Him this week? What will you receive in exchange?

02 What "aha!" moments or chapter highlights stood out to you this week?

03 What three next steps can you take as you continue making exchanges with God?

03. CONFESSION AND SURRENDER

"WHEN I KEPT SILENT, MY BONES WASTED AWAY
THROUGH MY GROANING ALL DAY LONG.."
PSALM 32:3

VIDEO NOTES

03. CONFESSION AND SURRENDER

My First Cry for Help

As you've heard, I struggled with drug addiction for many years. I was good at keeping it "under control," which really meant I was good at pretending my life was not spiraling out of control. However, everything came to a head one night while I was sitting under a bridge with my then boyfriend (I know, so cliché). We had been up for several days, high on meth, and were talking about what it would be like if we lived together – since, you know, we were so mature and ready for that (insert eye roll emoji). As we discussed our options in a drug-induced stupor, it suddenly dawned on me that I was supposed to take my dad to the airport so he could go to a job interview in San Diego. I raced out of there, hoping to not let my dad down once again.

On the drive there, I felt ashamed, exhausted, and emotional. I was overwhelmed with the sense that this was my chance to reach out and get help. If my dad got the job for which he was interviewing, he would leave and I would be stuck in a life steeped in drugs and darkness, and with a boyfriend who had no ability to truly love me. I knew if I stayed in my hometown, I probably would be dead soon.

The fear of being honest with my dad felt debilitating. I just kept thinking of how I had hurt him for so long, and how I had embarrassed him and brought shame upon my family. I wondered if he'd even help me. After all, I deserved for him to turn me away for all I had put him and my family through. Somehow, we made it to the airport on time. As we were pulling out his luggage, there was a VERY LARGE voice inside my brain that kept saying,

"SAY SOMETHING!" (God has never used any kind of still, quiet voice with me!) At the entrance of the airport, we just stood there, looking at each other. "SAY SOMETHING, ANYTHING!," my mind screamed. I took my glasses off and the look on his face said everything. You see, when you have been high and awake for several days, you DO NOT look good. Here I was, my daddy's little girl, destroyed by drugs, with my beauty hidden behind dark circles and gaunt cheeks.

He started to cry, big daddy tears streamed down his face. He knew I was in trouble and had known for a long time, but the evidence in front of him was unavoidable. All I could muster up in that moment was, "Dad, I need help." I waited for the condemnation, the lecture, or the stipulations for his help. Surprisingly, those never came. He just said, "Karrie, I love you. I will help you and I will never let you fall again."

As I drove away from the airport, I knew my life was going to change. A flicker of hope rose up in me. I hadn't felt that in so long. I knew my dad couldn't possibly prevent me from ever hurting again, but I knew that God was using my dad to send a message that was impossible for me to hear from Him at the time. My Heavenly Father used someone I knew loved me to speak hope into my life. I will never forget that moment, and I will never forget knowing deep within me that God was making a way for my healing.

Confessing to my dad and God that I needed help was an essential step I needed to take. I had to admit that I needed help, because you can't get help if you're not honest that you need it. Healing begins with reaching out and opening up to someone else.

CONFESSING TO OTHERS

NASB /

Furthermore, if two lie down together they keep warm, but how can one be warm alone? And if one can overpower him who is alone, two can resist him. A cord of three strands is not quickly torn apart.
Ecclesiastes 4:12

God often speaks of unity in the Bible. He talks about the body of Christ working together for ministry, accountability, and encouragement. He doesn't mention this once, but several times. In this way, it seems like God is saying, "HEY, listen up! This is important, so pay attention!"

God knew it wasn't good for man to be alone (Genesis 2:18). He created us with a need for companionship. This blows my mind! Adam walked with Jesus, but God still knew that Adam needed a partner. I see this being more about intimacy, accountability, and companionship, rather than just a need for a spouse. This was important for the very first human being, and it's still important for us today!

Reaching out to my father was a necessary step for my healing. With God's power (trust me, my dad needed it to love me; I was a doozy!), and my dad's love for me, he was able to help me out of the pit where I was living. Accountability is so important and companionship is essential to walking out of your hurt. I often say that we were not meant to be islands. Islands are easily bombed, but continents are HARD to take out. DON'T BE AN ISLAND! One of the many tactics of Satan is to isolate his prey. In John 10:10, we learn that he wants to kill, steal, and destroy. Just like a predator going after prey in the wild, Satan seeks out the weak, isolates them, and then attacks until they are rendered useless. On the other hand, the ones that stay with the herd are far less likely to get taken out. This couldn't be truer for us. We need a herd! We need to fight through the voices that urge us to isolate – they aren't from God!

I know this is hard to understand if people in your life have not proven themselves as trustworthy – maybe they have hurt or betrayed you. But, there are people out there who love you and are ready and willing to know what's really going on, and want to help. Reach out to them! God uses His people to minister to each other. He knows that sometimes you need a hug, some words of encouragement, or a "Girl, you goin' crazzzzy!" chat. This is why it is so important to step out and share your story.

NIV/

> *Therefore, confess your sins to each other and pray for each other so that you may be healed. The prayer of a righteous person is powerful and effective.*
> **James 5:16**

Secrets keep us locked up. They allow lies to fester and become truth. I can't reiterate this enough: when thoughts are left unspoken, they allow lies to swirl around in our heads, causing us to remain in bondage through the power they hold in our minds. The moment we confess our secrets, we shed light on the darkness they bring. Lies must be exposed, or they will continue to have too much power in our lives.

I know sharing your junk can be terrifying. However, if you really want to get better, this is not negotiable. You and I both know we are no good on our own. Our thoughts betray us, our feelings dictate what we do (which is always a slippery slope), and no matter how hard we try on our own, we are just not as strong by ourselves.

Pray that God brings women into your life who will honor Him in what they say.

This DOES NOT mean you have to tell the whole world all your junk! Just choose a few close confidants. This could be a trusted group, friend, therapist, life coach, or a pastor. Talk to someone YOU KNOW will help you get better, not just make you FEEL better.

These crucial conversations with women who love God and point you toward Him in love will help you see God in new ways, and that will help you feel stronger and able to heal. I do want to encourage you, though, to choose wisely, because not everyone is a worthy source of accountability. Pray that God brings women into your life who will honor Him in what they say. It's important to surround yourself with women who will point you to truth, even when it's difficult, and who will do it with love.

JOURNAL REFLECTION

Reflect on and respond to the following questions:

What causes you to isolate from others?

What is preventing you from reaching out to a trusted friend or community?

Is there someone in your life who will join you as you begin the process of accountability? If yes, who? Pray that God reveals the right person with whom you can share.

What benefits do you think will come from sharing your story?

CONFESSING TO GOD

Cast your cares on the LORD and He will sustain you; He will never let the righteous be shaken. **Psalm 55:22**

God loves you and He wants to heal you! But because we weren't created to be robots fully controlled by God, you have a choice. For you to be able to start down the road to healing, confessing before the Lord and allowing Him to minister to you is equally as important as sharing with a trusted confidant. You have never been in a safer place than when you allow God to invade your story.

If we confess our sins, He is faithful and just and will forgive us our sins and purify us from all unrighteousness. **1 John 1:9**

The moment you accepted Christ as your Savior, you were forgiven of past, present, and future sins. Confessing before the Lord is not as much about asking for forgiveness as it is about acknowledging and confessing sin. When we confess before the Lord, He can then remove the guilt of our past and the pain we carry. Confessing to God allows Him to enter places of your heart that have been blocked.

It's crazy to think that God loves you so much that He won't force you to choose Him. Think about that! He could just make you come to Him (I mean, He is God). Instead, He allows you to choose Him or not. It must break His heart to see His children in such pain from holding on to guilt and shame, knowing that if we would open our hearts to healing and surrender the pain, then He could actually do what He does best – REMOVE IT!

CONFESSION BREEDS INTIMACY

It's common to put confession in the same category as forgiveness, but this is not where it lives. When Jesus died on the cross and you accepted this free gift, you were forgiven of past, present, and future sins. This was the whole point of the cross!

With confession, it is less about asking for forgiveness and more of an invitation to God into your pain. God will not bombard His way into your heart; He will patiently await your invitation. The surrender that comes from this invitation will produce intimacy with your Father and allow for continued trust in offering your confession to Him.

 NIV

When I kept silent, my bones wasted away through my groaning all day long. For day and night Your hand was heavy on me; my strength was sapped as in the heat of summer. Then I acknowledged my sin to You and did not cover up my iniquity. I said, 'I will confess my transgressions to the Lord.' And You forgave the guilt of my sin.
Psalm 32:3-5

As we understand David's story, we see that it was the silence or the secret he carried that kept him in turmoil and put a wall up between him and the Lord. The reference I made was that it is as if we have this box in our heart, a box filled with secrets and shame. It's not just enough to acknowledge the box is there, we must open it up and confess it before the Lord so we can have restored intimacy.

EXERCISE
Restoring Intimacy

What secrets have you been storing in your heart's box?

There is power in confession and beauty in the restored intimacy thatis waiting for you.

James 4:7-10 clearly illustrates the steps for confession and restored intimacy:

"Submit yourselves, then, to God.
Resist the devil, and He will flee from
you. Come near to God and He will
come near to you. Wash your hands,
you sinners, and purify your hearts,
you double-minded. Grieve, mourn
and wail. Change your laughter to
mourning and your joy to gloom.
Humble yourselves before the Lord,
and He will exalt you."

There is so much I want to say about this verse. It is so rich in steps for healing, but I want to focus on one area that I believe is vital to restored intimacy with God. He says to "grieve, mourn, and wail. Change your laughter to mourning and your joy to gloom." You may think, "WHY? This sounds depressing." God wants you to come to Him and lay your burdens at His feet. He knows that keeping it locked inside will never allow you to experience freedom. There needs to be brokenness over your pain and sin. When you come to Him with a heart of repentance and a need for healing, then, and only then, will your relationship with God be restored. The verse continues to state that, when we are humbled before the Lord – which actually means leveled before Him – He can exalt you. This is so opposite of what we think today. We have the mindset that we need to get it together before we come to God or we will be completely judged. There are so many verses that show us how completely untrue this is!

Yes, you do need to repent, you do need to surrender, and you do need to be broken about where you are and what you have done. However, it doesn't end there! In fact, it begins there!

When all this is said and done, Jesus comes in, removes the guilt and shame, and you are EXALTED! God wants all of His children to soar, not to be bogged down with their sin and shame. He wants you to be free, but you have to do your part.

No more island-living, no more secrets, and no more wasting away. It's time to confess before the Lord what has been keeping you from Him. When you do this, you will see how beautifully the Lord comes in and restores your heart unto Him. The healing that will take place will blow your mind!

JOURNAL REFLECTION

It's time to write out your confession before the Lord. It helps to get these thoughts out in writing. It also is helpful for you to reflect back on this in times when you start to try and "take back the backpack." If you are not sure what you need to confess, ask God to reveal it.

If you don't hear it right away, continue to ask. He will let you know, because He desires for you to be close to Him.

Ask yourself questions like "What do I need to confess before the Lord?" or "What value will come from confessing to God?". (Psalm 55:22). Seek answers and He will help you find them.

"

*GOD WANTS
ALL OF HIS
CHILDREN TO
SOAR, NOT TO
BE BOGGED
DOWN WITH
THEIR SIN
AND SHAME.*

SURRENDER

UGH! Surrender is such a hard word! Maybe you are thinking, "If I give up this hurt, then what will I have? Who will I be?" For many of you, although you desperately want to be free, this pain has become far too comfortable. Giving up control means you now have to deal with YOU! This can be terrifying, BUT God desires all of you to be healed and free! You know as well as I do that partial surrender does not result in true healing. It's time to lay down control and surrender before the Lord.

Confession and surrender must go hand in hand. To truly experience the freedom that comes from confessing your sin, you must also surrender your pain and sin to the Lord. This also means releasing the reins of your life to Him.

You live in defeat when you try to control your life. You don't know what's best for you because your grid is skewed. Your feelings have dictated your actions for far too long. Jesus Christ is the only one who can fix all of that! He CANNOT heal you until you relinquish control. Jesus wants to invade your story and bring life and freedom to it.

NLT / *If you try to hang on to your life, you will lose it. But if you give up your life for My sake, you will save it.* **Matthew 16:25**

Holding on to our junk gives a false sense of security. Trying to control our life will ultimately cause us to lose it. We may not physically die, but possibly emotionally, spiritually, and maybe even socially. It's not worth it.

When you allow God to invade your story, you begin to go from victim to victory.

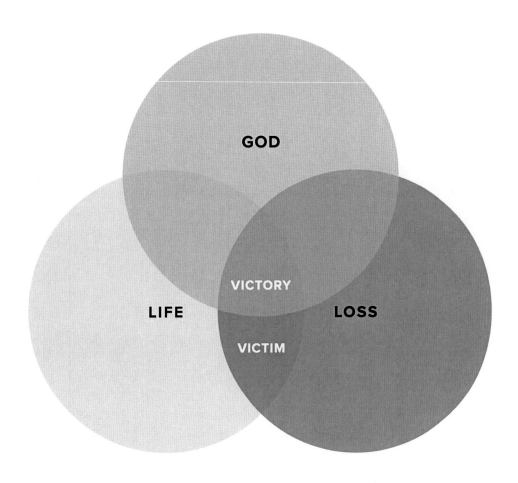

EXERCISE
Surrendering to God

PART ONE:

Find a place where you can pray privately and OUT LOUD (there is purpose in this). Sometimes, we need to verbalize a statement that is critical to changing the way we see ourselves. When you have found that place, pray a prayer of surrender aloud. You can say your own or you can say the one below.

Lord, I surrender my _____ to you. I no longer want this to be a secret in my life. My desire is for You to take control of this area and for You to fill my heart with truth and healing. I have ignored _____ for too long and I no longer want it to have power over me. Help me, Lord, to remember this moment. When I start to live back in the shame, remind me of this prayer of surrender and restore me back to a place of peace. You are my God and I am Your daughter; I will trust You with my pain, and I will walk surrendered to who You say I am. Amen.

PART TWO:

Read this passage and underline the words in the verse that stand out to you.

Come to Me, all who labor and are heavy laden, and I will give you rest. Take My yoke upon you, and learn from Me, for I am gentle and lowly in heart, and you will find rest for your souls. For My yoke is easy, and My burden is light.
Matthew 11:28-30

What is this verse saying to you?

How would it feel to surrender your life to God?

Pray and ask God to reveal areas of your life that He wants you to turn over to Him. Don't underestimate the small things; sometimes it's the smallest things that keep us from being truly set free. Write out what He is saying to you.

WEEKLY BIG 3

01 **What is God asking you to release to Him this week? What will you receive in exchange?**

What "aha!" moments or chapter highlights stood out to you this week? *02*

03 **What three next steps can you take as you continue making exchanges with God?**

04. GRIEVING

"A TIME TO WEAP AND A TIME TO LAUGH,
A TIME TO MOURN AND A TIME TO DANCE."
ECCLESIASTES 3:4

VIDEO NOTES

04. GRIEVING

The world will tell you there are two ways to react to pain: "Be tough, bury your feelings, and move on!", or "Own your pain and make it your identity." However, NEITHER brings healing. The key is to not let what has happened become your identity, but the opposite – ignoring or burying it – only brings bondage to it! Allowing yourself to identify your pain and to grieve are essential parts of healing. God wants you to acknowledge your hurt before Him and understand that there is a time for every season.

ESV /
> *Blessed are those who mourn, for they*
> *shall be comforted. **Matthew 5:4***

Grieving what has been lost or taken from you is essential to moving forward. It is NOT WEAKNESS, it actually is strength. It takes bravery to face what has hurt you. Grieving the shattered expectations you had or the pain of your mistakes allows you to cleanse from deep within, and it gives you the ability to move forward. With unresolved bitterness and anger, darkness erodes our hearts and freedom cannot take place.

Take care when grieving from pain you've experienced, though. Many find comfort in staying stuck in this process, as they feel justified in their hurt (often rightfully so), and don't want to leave that place.

GRIEF IN MY LIFE

As a little girl, I grew up knowing that my mom was not healthy. I knew she loved me the best she could, but I also knew she was deeply hurt. For years, I watched as the pain of her life continued to become her identity. She would frequently say how fat she was — despite that she often weighed less than 100 pounds. I also sensed her feelings of failure when it came to raising me and my sister. Watching this person I loved waste away because of the many lies she believed about herself was heart wrenching. It caused me to act out in ways that were destructive and really made me want to retreat from anything that was good. I wanted her to step up and be the mom I needed her to be so badly. Unfortunately, this dream never came true.

As my mom struggled with an eating disorder and mental illness for years, I watched someone who once had life and vitality wither away into a shell of a person. When I was 30 years old, the lies that my mom told herself finally took their toll. She couldn't take one more day of mental torture here on earth. One night, she decided everyone would be better off without her.

My mom's suicide was one of the worst moments of my life. I was so hurt and angry. I couldn't believe she was gone. So many of the wounds I was carrying were hurts from my childhood — wounds I had to work hard to try to put behind me. I tried to just move on, but the grief was manifesting itself in other ways, including depression and anxiety. Her death triggered many of the unresolved hurts I was holding on to, and I knew I needed help. As I sought wise counsel, one of the my biggest breakthroughs was realizing the necessity of grieving.

...grieving what has been lost or taken from you is essential to moving forward...

At first, grieving seemed pointless. I wanted to move on to the healing and fixing, but the hurt, pain, and shame I was holding on to was keeping me stuck. So I began the VERY arduous task of sitting in my pain! I allowed myself to be angry and then hurt. I let go of the many expectations I had for my life and for what a mom was supposed to be like. As this process took place, I could feel the anger with my mom start to fade and I began to see her through the grid of God's love for her and the pain she carried all those years.

I have never once thought that the way she treated me was ok, but the grace I began to have for her by acknowledging my own pain helped me to love her and release the hold her actions had on my life. I grieved for the mom I wanted, and I grieved for the loss she brought. I grieved my childhood, my lack of nurturing, how much I missed her, and I grieved that she was now gone. After doing the hard work of identifying my pain, the way it had affected me, and the way it had played out in my life, peace started to fill my heart.

I want you to know that grieving was an essential part of getting me closer to a place of forgiveness and allowed me to eventually release the pain of my past.

DON'T FEAR GRIEF

I'm sure there are a few fears that come up when contemplating going into the grieving process. You may be afraid that if you grieve and then move on, what has happened will be forgotten or the action will somehow be justified. This is just NOT true. Grieving and then healing from that grief does not change what has happened, but it frees you to allow these past hurts to no longer define you. By grieving, you allow yourself the ability to move on and remove the power from what happened or how it made you feel, and you will then start to move forward and into new thoughts and new actions.

You may also be afraid that you'll never be able to function with the sadness that will surface if you allow yourself to feel the pain you've experienced. However, just because you are not walking around crying all the time doesn't mean you're doing a good job at keeping it together. Grieving frees those emotions that are buried deep inside you, and, by getting them out, you now have the ability to grieve what has been lost and to then move forward into healing.

I totally get it. There is so much fear in "going there," in allowing yourself to truly feel the hurt that you have caused or that has been inflicted on you. You might be thinking, "Why bring up all that pain again? If I start crying, I will never stop! What if I open myself up again and I can't keep it together?" There are so many fears we are plagued with, but allow me to share this truth with you: Satan does not want you to deal with this, because he does not want you to be free. His desire is for you to keep your hurts inside where they fester and eat away at you until you become a shell of a person.

JOURNAL REFLECTION

Grieving is a powerful part of the healing process, but only when we grieve with purpose. As you look at the chart on the next page, you will see the typical response to grief compared to healthy, biblical process of grieving.

The biblical response to grieving is not to take the place of the typical response, but rather to accompany it. For example, when we are wounded, our natural response is to be in denial or to isolate. Moving from the natural response to the biblical one, you move towards comfort and healing. In the midst of your denial, you will need to get really honest about what you are feeling — to become aware of the feelings you are experiencing. This will be a powerful first step to moving towards the next step.

Take some time to look over the chart, then process some of your grief through these grids. Read the scripture to give you courage, then answer the questions on the next page. This will be a valuable tool for the rest of your life. I still use this and need to be aware of where I am in the grieving process when encountering pain. This can be a good heart check to see where you may be stuck and to allow the biblical model to come in and help heal what has been broken.

STAGE	TYPICAL GRIEF RESPONSE	BIBLICAL GRIEF RESPONSE
01	DENIAL / ISOLATION	**CANDOR: Honesty with myself.** Psalm 51:6 (ESV) Psalm 25:16 (ESV)
02	ANGER / RESENTMENT	**COMPLAINT: Honesty with God.** Psalm 6:3-6 (ESV), Psalm 13:2 (ESV)
03	BARGAINING / WORKS	**CRY: Asking God for help.** Hebrews 4:16 (NLT) Psalm 40:1-2 (NLT)
04	DEPRESSION / ALIENATION	**COMFORT: Receiving God's help.** Psalm 46:1 (ESV) Isaiah 41:10 (NASB)
05	ACCEPTANCE / RESOLUTION *(typical response ends here)*	**CASTING: Surrendering the hurt.** 1 Peter 5:6-7 (NLT) Psalm 55:22 (MSG)
06	——————————————	**CALLED: Using your past pain to help others.** Luke 8:39 (ESV) Isaiah 61:3-7 (MSG)

What are some of the fears you have about grieving?

Although there may be fear, what value do you think will come from grieving?

What encourages you about the way God has called us to grieve as opposed to the way the world says to grieve?

Where do you see yourself stuck in the grieving process?

When hearing the story of Jesus grieving in the garden, what encouragement were you able to take for yourself in relation to your grieving?

GRIEF AND YOUR BRAIN

Bear with me, we're going to get scientific for a minute... (Well, as scientific as a I can be.) Understanding how your brain manages emotional trauma further supports how important grief is to your healing process. The brain is an interesting organ; its abilities go far beyond what man has been able to study. One thing we know is that the brain will always try to make sense of, or at least cope with, a tragic situation. Tragedy can range from a childhood spent feeling unseen or unworthy in your house, to rape or molestation. The hurts you carry are stored in that miraculous brain of yours, and without giving words to the hurt and allowing yourself to grieve, they remain locked in your brain. When this happens, the pain has power over you and it becomes the grid through which you view your life.

As your brain tries to cope with the pain, it goes into survival mode and begins compartmentalizing all those feelings. Don't be mistaken though, as the pain is still very much there. These "put away" emotions have a huge impact on you today. The goal in life is to thrive, not just survive!

GOD WILL COMFORT YOU

 ESV

Humble yourselves, therefore, under the mighty hand of God so that at the proper time He may exalt you, casting all your anxieties on Him, because He CARES for you.
1 Peter 5:6-7, Emphasis Added

God's Word is very clear on how important it is to grieve and how much He is with you in the grieving process. God is not only the greatest healer, He is also the BEST comforter. There often is an expectation that grieving and allowing ourselves to "go there" will automatically be met with comfort and healing. Grieving takes time, though, and healing takes even longer. God isn't saying that the pain will go away instantly when you mourn, but rather, He is saying that He will be with you every step of the way. You are not alone in this and you will be delivered in time!

In order to receive comfort, you must enter into grief, sit in it, and allow God to comfort you. Your brain was not made to hold the power of grief. When you allow yourself to be open about the hurts you have, God can come in and comfort what has been causing you pain. When trapped in your brain, there is no avenue for you to let God enter in and heal. Grieving is essential!

You might be afraid that God won't comfort you when or how you want Him to. You may be wondering, "What if I am sad forever?" or "What if I can't get past all this pain?"

"

LET ME ASSURE YOU, GOD'S WORD PROMISES THAT HE WILL MEET YOU.

Trust that the Lord will guide you and exalt you in the right time. He really does know what's best for you. God doesn't want to rush your healing because that doesn't help you. He knows the exact amount of time you need to sit with something. Don't rush through grieving just so you don't have to feel sad anymore. It is so critical that you allow the Holy Spirit to guide you through this process so you learn all you need to learn and heal completely from the burdens you have been carrying.

EXERCISE
Comfort Through Pain

NIV /

Blessed are those who mourn, for they shall be comforted. **Matthew 5:4**

As you read this scripture, what is God saying must happen in order for you to be comforted?

What truths for your life can you take from this scripture?

What promise can you hold on to for your own grief?

What is the result when we come under the mighty hand of God?

What is the amount of time God says it will take to experience freedom from the hurts you carry?

Read Psalm 69:13-18. *(The psalmist is one of the best grievers I have ever seen. In fact, all of Psalms meets me in my drama like no other book of the Bible – I'm in it often!)* **What stands out to you about how David grieves? How is this different from how you grieve?**

BEGINNING THE GRIEVING PROCESS

Here are some important tips when entering into your grieving process:

Make sure you are in some kind of support group or community group. It is important to make sure you are sharing your thoughts and hurts with someone. Remember, it's not good for man – or woman – to be alone!

Pray. It is so important to take your grief before the Lord. It's ok if you're mad at Him (He can take it), but don't try to grieve without the power of the Holy Spirit guiding you. As I said before, Satan's only goal is to take you out, and he will try to turn what started as a good thing into something that makes you more stuck. Press into the healing power of scripture and prayer. This also would be a good time to revisit church if you aren't already going (if you need recommendations, we can help with that).

See a counselor if your grieving brings up huge wounds of violation or is causing you to think harmful thoughts that are taking you to extremely dark places. Finding a Christian counselor is incredibly important. The Holy Spirit must be in the room to speak to the counselor and to your heart for true healing to take place. There is NO shame in counseling. I attribute much of my healing to the many years of counseling I have gone through.

Finally, as you begin to allow yourself to grieve, don't forget for one minute that God is in the business of delivering people from their pain. He's been doing it since THE BEGINNING OF TIME. If you're struggling to believe that God can heal you, that He's with you, or that He will never leave you, just remember that He saved Israel from Egypt, raised Jesus from the dead, and healed the deeply wounded – He can help you in your time of despair!

It is so important to take your grief before the Lord. It's okay if you're mad at Him (He can take it), but don't try to grieve without the power of the Holy Spirit guiding you.

EXERCISE
Preparing to Grieve

Grieving is important, so I want to give you a healthy way to process through some of your grief. You MUST get the hurt out of your brain. The thoughts you are wrestling with are like wrecking balls for your mind. They are wreaking havoc and keeping you stuck. It's time to purge and grieve. Don't be afraid – I promise it will be the most cleansing step you have taken! The exchange that happens when we grieve in a healthy way allows grief to have its proper place. When we grieve this way, God's peace is then able to come in and heal the wounded places.

What feelings come up when you think of going through the process of grieving?

What fears do you have about entering into grieving?

What fears do you have about grieving? What hurts do you need to start grieving? *(If you are having a hard time pinpointing what it is God wants to free you from, pray that He reveals this to you.)*

Read Psalm 40:1-3. What are the results of crying out to God?

JOURNAL REFLECTION

Write a letter TO your pain. (Remember I mentioned I did this? It helps, I promise.) Write down everything that has been taken, expectations that have been lost, and even specifics of the hurt that you have experienced. This may be about a particular person or event. Write about it and get it out. Don't hold back. Write about what your life has looked like with this hurt in it. What has this pain robbed from you? How has it changed you? Has this change affected any loved ones? Try to find words to express this pain. Not only "I am angry" or "I am scared," but try to find what is behind those feelings.

If you are angry, what feeling is behind the anger? Is it hurt or fear?

Try to express what's going on deep in your heart, not just your initial gut reaction to life or this situation. This is important in grieving. You must find out what is driving your grief and how it is affecting you on a deeper level. You will not have to publicly share what you wrote. However, it may be good to share these thoughts with a counselor or a trusted friend. You may need prayer, a hug, or wise counsel on how to navigate through this. After you are done writing and you have gotten EVERYTHING out, PRAY! Pray for release of this, for healing, and for truth to start to come in. Allow God to meet you in your grief. Ask Him to comfort you and help you begin releasing the hold that these incidents have on your life.

Once you do that, it's time to start the process of releasing this grief. This may take a while. Pray again that God will start to help you release these thoughts. Take this week to really dive into God's Word, listen to some good worship music, and pray with friends. Surround yourself with the presence of the Lord, and ask specifically for God to meet you in this pain. He will!

Grieving can be ongoing. Be kind to yourself; when needed, stop and allow yourself to grieve with a prayer of surrender. Some wounds never fully heal, but when you properly grieve, the hurts won't have the power over you they once had and God's peace will become more readily available.

WEEKLY BIG 3

01
___

What is God asking you to release to Him this week? What will you receive in exchange?

02
___

What "aha!" moments or chapter highlights stood out to you this week?

03
___

What three next steps can you take as you continue making exchanges with God?

05. SOUL CARE

"WHAT GOOD WILL IT BE FOR SOMEONE TO
GAIN THE WHOLE WORLD, YET FORFEIT
THEIR SOUL? OR WHAT CAN ANYONE GIVE
IN EXCHANGE FOR THEIR SOUL?"
MATTHEW 16:26

VIDEO NOTES

05. SOUL CARE

When creating this course, I never intended to have a section on soul care. In fact, I knew I wanted to have a break after grieving, but I was going to address this section as Be Brave — encouraging you to keep going and to be brave. Let me tell you, I am so glad God loves you more than I ever could and has spoken so clearly about every single topic I write about. He spoke to my heart early one morning and said, "Karrie, they don't need to be more brave, they already are brave. They need to rest!" A light bulb came on because not only was He asking me to change an entire week's topic, He had been speaking this to me for almost six months. I felt the heaviness so many of you carry; I immediately saw all of us women scrambling around trying to do it all and be it all. I could hear the kindness of God speaking over all of us that He does not want us to strive and become worn out. He wants us filled by His Spirit so that we can accomplish all that is in front of us. Our Father is kind, and He wants you to be kind to yourself.

WHEN WAS THE LAST TIME YOU DID SOMETHING REJUVENATING AND HOW DID IT MAKE YOU FEEL?

WHAT KEEPS YOU FROM TAKING TIME
FOR YOURSELF ON A REGULAR BASIS?

WHATEVER IS KEEPING YOU FROM TAKING CARE OF
YOURSELF, DO YOU THINK IT IS JUST AN EXCUSE?

This week, you are asked to rest. Now, as I shared in the video, rest does not mean numb out. To care for your soul is to find something that rejuvenates you. I will ask you to commit to one, two, or three activities that will bring life to your weary bones. My hope is that you will choose to do three!

Here is the only rule: whatever you choose needs to actually fill your spirit, so that when you are done you feel lighter, you can breathe more deeply. Maybe you have never done something like this and are wondering, "How do I know what will fill my soul?" Well, it may be trial and error at first, and that's okay. Consider being alone for at least one or two of your activities. Often, getting outside and being still is fulfilling.

HERE ARE A FEW THINGS TO TRY:

- Go to the beach.

- Go on a walk.

- Lay in the grass.

- Listen to music.

- Practice breathing and stretching.

- Sit in meditation (where you fill your spirit with the presence of God).

- Grab coffee with a good friend.

- Listen to a pastor's message/sermon.

- Ask yourself, "what does my mind say?"

- Read the Word of God with no agenda except to soak in His goodness.

- Exercise.

- Listen to an encouraging podcast.

- Get a pedicure.

- Go on a hike.

- Go on a date night.

- Snuggle on the bed with **ONE** of your kiddos. *(You may have to do this with each so they don't get jealous, but this is a great time for you and for them.)*

- Take a road trip somewhere you've always wanted to go.

I could go on and on and please feel free to add your own, but this is a good place to start. Regardless of what you choose to do during your soul care time, ask yourself these questions:

What am I feeling?

What am I fearing?

Is there something I believe about myself or God that is keeping me from allowing Him into the fragile places of my heart?

PSALM 62:1

"TRULY MY SOUL
FINDS REST IN GOD,
MY SALVATION
COMES FROM HIM."

In order to pour out,
you must be poured into.

In the long run, I hope that taking time for soul care becomes your new normal, and that you are able to feel the unrest so deeply that you KNOW it's time to stop. I believe if you can set goals for soul care, ALL you want to accomplish will be much easier and SO much more rewarding!

Write out some soul care goals in the four sections below. Daily soul care is something free or of little cost. Your yearly care may require more investment.

DAILY:

WEEKLY:

MONTHLY:

YEARLY:

NOW CLOSE THIS BOOK AND GO TAKE CARE OF YOU!

WEEKLY BIG 3

01 **What is God asking you to release to Him this week? What will you receive in exchange?**

What "aha!" moments or chapter highlights stood out to you this week? *02*

03 **What three next steps can you take as you continue making exchanges with God?**

06. TRUST

"TRUST IN THE LORD WITH ALL YOUR HEART
AND LEAN NOT ON YOUR OWN UNDERSTANDING;
IN ALL YOUR WAYS SUBMIT TO HIM, AND HE
WILL MAKE YOUR PATHS STRAIGHT."
PROVERBS 3:5-6

VIDEO NOTES

06. TRUST

Trust is a tricky word. The dictionary defines it as "the firm belief in the reliability, truth, ability, or strength of someone or something." Although we throw it around all the time, this tiny word carries a huge amount of weight. Saying "I trust you" means a great deal in today's society, because the world is filled with people who act in an untrustworthy manner. We see this in politics, relationships, churches, businesses...the list could go on.

Because of this, it's not surprising that many of us have a hard time when it comes to trusting God. We have seen nothing but untrustworthy behavior in almost every aspect of our lives. However, God asks us to trust Him with our whole hearts. I get it, it's difficult to trust Him when we can't trust anyone around us – and when we can't even trust ourselves. Here's the exciting thing, though: God wants to blow your mind in this area. He wants you to see that His love for you IS trustworthy and you NEED to trust Him to truly be free.

Just like chapter four, this one is more interactive than the first few. I encourage you, again, to take your time as you work through this. Building trust is incredibly important, so I hope you'll devote the necessary time to complete each of the exercises and answer all of the questions.

EXERCISE
Distrust is Isolating

I'd like you to draw your own version of the box I drew in this week's video. My hope is that this exercise will demonstrate how isolation becomes our home and what it looks like when fear causes us to miss out on the life God has for us.

1. **Draw a box. This represents your home.**

2. **Draw a person in the box. This person represents you.**

3. **Decorate the inside of your box, using color where and how you want. Is there a couch, tv, pictures, etc.?**

4. **Draw a sun outside of the box, with rays coming down all over the top of the box.**

5. **Around the box, I want you to draw a place that brings you joy. This could be the beach, the mountains, a field with flowers, etc. Take some time to do this. Use color! (Trust me, I'm not an artsy person, but it helps with the exercise to add color!)**

6. **Now, with a light hand, I want you to take the black or grey pencil and lightly color all over the inside of your box.**

This is your life when you don't trust anyone. You control your surroundings. You don't let anyone in. You have made a home for yourself in this box. You have said to yourself, "If I just stay in here, I can't get hurt anymore." You believe this so deeply that you fight with full resistance to avoid letting anyone into your box. You have lived your whole life in this box, living behind fear, anger, hurt, resentment, and shame. Maybe you have allowed people to visit you inside this space only to be hurt by them, confirming that, indeed, people cannot be trusted! You lock the door, shut all the windows and dive deeper and deeper into loneliness. This only leaves you further isolated from real interaction. This is no way to live, and this is the antithesis of freedom.

Many of you are asking, "WHY should I get out of the box?! Honestly, it's comfortable in here! I have it decorated, hung a few pictures. I even let people visit every once in a while. I am comfortable here." To this, I respond that true freedom can't come until we surrender our junk before God and TRUST Him to heal it. We are wounded, fragile creatures. We do NOT have the ability to heal ourselves, NOR do we have the ability to heal those around us. Many of us have tried, and have failed miserably. For far too long, we have believed the lie that if we conceal our stuff, somehow it will just go away. So, we stay trapped in a box, thinking, "Well, I guess this is the best it ever will be."

God can't heal you until you choose to hand over your pain and hurts, truly surrendering control, and then trusting Him to heal what is broken. I know this is easier said than done, but trust is mandatory for living in freedom.

Now, ask yourself the following questions:

What did I learn about myself from this exercise?

What fears do I have about stepping out of the box?

What benefits would come from stepping out of my box?

A TRUST LIKE JESUS

Even Jesus had to know His Father was good and had to step into a trust relationship with Him. During our week on grieving, we discussed how Jesus grieved deeply in the Garden of Gethsemane the night before He was crucified (Matthew 26:36-45). We read about His anguish and how He wanted to "let this pass from [Him], if possible." Jesus knew that His Father was good. He knew that He could trust His Dad with His life. As He wept in the garden, praying to have a different option, something happened in that third time of prayer. We don't know what was said, but what we do see is that Jesus' countenance changed. He walked back over to the disciples, ready to accept His fate. What made Jesus go from weeping tears of blood to a state of full surrender and peace? TRUST!

The crazy part is Jesus' actual circumstance didn't change — there was no other way than for Jesus to die on the cross — but He had peace that He didn't have before. God, His Father, reached in and comforted Him in His pain, and Jesus responded with surrender and trust. This trust in His Father allowed Him to not only face the most difficult and painful moment of His life, but He also was able to face it with peace and surrender. After this moment, we never again see Jesus break down like this. He never yells or lashes out in anger. In fact, He is so calm it almost brings anger to the fighter in me. I think, "Yell something! Fight back!" (Just one more reason I am NOT God!) Jesus knew this was the only way, so He had to surrender to what His Father asked of Him. Jesus trusted that this act would enable all of creation to be restored, and He trusted that He soon would be free of this temporary pain.

Jesus would not have been able to go into this battle without knowing the heart of His Father. He knew the goodness, kindness, and trustworthiness of His Dad, and, through that, He was able to endure pain and even death.

EXERCISE
Trust in the Bible

The Bible is filled with scriptures on trust, because GOD WANTS YOU TO KNOW THAT THIS IS IMPORTANT TO HIM! Take a look at the verses below and write what you feel God is revealing to you about trust.

JEREMIAH 17:7-8

ISAIAH 43:2

HEBREWS 13:6

PSALM 18:2

2 SAMUEL 22:31

MATTHEW 16:25

As you have read, God is FOR YOU! He loves you and He IS trustworthy!

Reflect on what you just read and answer the questions below.

What are some characteristics of a trustworthy person?

What are three (or more) areas of your life, based on what you have seen or experienced, that show God is trustworthy?

What do you do when you feel at the end of your rope?

In your deepest hurt, where do you turn? Has it helped?

How different would your life be if you fully trusted God?

What is keeping you from trusting God?

SURRENDERING CONTROL

I want to take a moment to share about the word "control." If you're like me, you probably love control and don't like feeling out of control. Perhaps thinking about releasing control breeds anxiety, fear, or anger. One definition of control is "the power to influence or direct people's behavior or the course of events." Nothing seems to be wrong with this definition. In fact, it sounds pretty awesome to me. I LOVE being in control! The problem, though, is that control is the complete opposite of trust.

All control is not bad, though, because we need to have some of it in areas of our lives. In fact, in Galatians 5:22, God tells us that self-control is evidence of the Spirit of God in our lives! The absence of self-control leads to utter chaos and destruction. But, what happens when we try to control the things that are not meant for us to control? We try to play God in our life or the lives of others, causing anxiety and fear.

You might think that controlling your surroundings, emotions, or even other people will somehow keep you from getting hurt. You may even mask your desire for control by putting it under the guise of protection, concern, strength, or other seemingly positive desires. When you do this, you fool yourself into thinking that this is freedom. The truth, though, is that you are not in control of anything outside of what YOU think and do.

Attempting to control areas beyond ourselves keeps us from truly trusting God. It also alienates us from Him, preventing true intimacy with Him. He cannot heal what is broken if you are busy trying to control how to fix it, how to feel about it, or how to avoid it.

EXERCISE
Control in Your Life

Identify an area of your life which you most often try to control, then
answer the questions below.

What fear do you have about letting go of this area of control?

Has your ability to control this area brought peace and healing to your heart?

What has been the outcome of trying to control your situation or feelings?

What freedom would come from surrendering control of this area to God?

JOURNAL REFLECTION

Reflect on areas in your life where you have trust issues. Write to the Lord about what it would look like to release control and allow trust to come in.

SURRENDERING CONTROL & TRUSTING GOD

So, how do you begin to surrender control and start trusting God? Trust takes practice. You will never know that God is trustworthy if you don't choose to trust Him. He wants you to hand over what hurts. He wants to be able to heal your heart. He wants you to walk in freedom, but you are not a robot, so He will not force you to hand over control. You must choose this for yourself.

HERE ARE SOME TIPS FOR LEARNING TO TRUST GOD:

/ Be honest. Acknowledge what is hurting you, or what frightens you. Just like when we are leaving a victim mindset behind, the same is true for when we are trying to learn how to trust: honesty is key! We can only attempt to heal in areas of which we are aware.

/ Ask God to take the hurt. You may have to do this repeatedly, and that's ok! You have been wounded and it is going to take time to heal. You have built up defenses to get through life, and now you are being asked to take them down. Expect resistance and fear to creep in. Remember that trust is not based on what we feel, but on what we know! Discipline your mind to stay focused on Christ and His healing, not on your fears.

/ Pray for healing. We don't do this enough. Instead, we plead with God to just remove the pain. Be specific about the wounds you need healed. Pray about exactly what is keeping you stuck – and don't stop praying!

/ Be patient. Healing takes a long time, but Jesus is faithful. Your timing is not His timing, but He is always good and knows what's best for you. This is where you will have to practice your trust in the Lord. If healing is taking longer than you want, or if it is not coming at all, this does not mean that God is not trustworthy. He is working out good in your life and will use all things for the betterment of your life – if you let Him.

THE FEAR FACTOR

For all who are led by the Spirit of God are sons of God. For you did not receive the spirit of slavery to fall back into fear, but you have received the Spirit of adoption as sons, by whom we cry, "Abba! Father!" **Romans 8:14-16**

The opposite of trust is fear; it keeps us stuck more than anything else we feel. Sometimes fear is good because it keeps us from doing dangerous things or putting ourselves in harmful situations. Often, however, the emotions of fear have way too much power in our actions and keep us from really living a life of victory.

Now that you know you are God's child, you do not have to fall back into a spirit of slavery or FEAR! You are adopted as children of GOD! When you understand who you are and the power that lives inside you, you will start to eradicate fear from your life. Claiming truth about who you are and WHOSE you are will be the very things that start to allow you to walk in power.

Satan has very few tricks. He is not creative. Yes, he's crafty, but he's not creative. He tends to use the same tactics over and over again, and his primary tool is fear. He wants you to believe that you can't trust God and that letting go of your hurts, having faith, surrendering your desires, and even stepping out in faith will result in a horrible life. This could not be further from the truth!

FAITH AND FEAR

LIKE A FOOL, I once decided to go bungee jumping. I thought this would somehow be a good way to usher in my 21st year of life. I should have just gone to a bar like most young adults seeking a rite of passage. Instead, I decided to test my fate and JUMP OFF a very high crane with nothing but straps attached to my ankles. As I climbed up this tower, the fear that started to come over my body was like nothing I had ever felt. I just kept thinking, "Why did I want to do this?" (Now, this is an example of when HEALTHY fear kicks in. Apparently, though, my whole life I had learned to ignore that little voice...) ANYWAY, I got to the top, and it was just me and the TEENAGE instructor standing up there. (Seriously, my life was in the hands of a pimply faced boy who had ZERO care whether I lived or died.) I looked down (I know... NEVER LOOK DOWN) and saw all my friends and family waving. "There is no way I can go back down," I thought. I asked the young boy about how this worked, what was going to happen, and if I was going to die. You know, the usual pre-bungee-jumping questions. He assured me that the cord attached to my ankles was very strong and they hadn't lost anyone...yet. YET?! Oh. Dear.

So, I stepped to the edge and turned around (I could NOT jump face first), then just stood there frozen in fear. There was no way I could do it. My body fought with everything in it – it would not allow me to go. I tried to get the instructor to push me, but apparently that was "against the rules." I didn't trust the cord or the ankle straps or the baby boy, so NOTHING at this point was trustworthy. Since I'm slightly competitive, I also knew that I could not handle the failure of not jumping. I mean, everyone was watching! So, as I stood there, I just said to myself, "Well God, I might be seeing you soon!" My body went limp like I was dead, and I just let go. I don't remember anything about the fall, but what I do VIVIDLY remember is the moment when the cord yanked and I was safe.

What a relief. IT WORKED! Their record of "no one has died...YET!" was still strong. The crazy part after all of this is that I don't fear bungee jumping anymore. I trust the ropes and the straps because I know that they work and that I will not get hurt (but for the record, I'm still reluctant about the man-child).

Sometimes to really get rid of fear, you have to have gut-wrenching faith. You have to believe that what God says is true. You can still be afraid – heck, I'm scared all the time – but I KNOW God will see me through. He has proven Himself over and over again. Trusting God and having faith in Him does not mean that there isn't fear, it means that you are able to move forward and step into the life He is calling you to live.

Fear without faith is DREAD. Dread is the yucky fear that makes you worry about outcomes or situations. Dread is what holds you back when God is asking you to let go of hurt, rejection, failure, unmet expectations, or even the unknown. Dread and faith can't coexist; they are like oil and water. Your trust, your FAITH, has to be BIGGER than your fear. God will give this to you, but you have to choose to trust Him. When you need to be encouraged, read Hebrews 11. You will see it was BY FAITH that amazing things happened. Many of these stories are filled with ill-equipped people who were scared to death, yet chose to TRUST that what God says is true.

In Joshua 1:9, He says, "Have I not commanded you? Be strong and courageous! Do not tremble or be dismayed, for the Lord your God is with you wherever you go." You do not go at this alone. You can trust Jesus and, as you step out in faith more and more, you will see His faithfulness and this will continue to build your trust in Him. You are in the safest hands you could ever be in, so let dreadful fear be put to rest in your life and trust your heavenly Father. He only wants GOOD for His children, even though sometimes that "good" looks differently than we think it should.

EXERCISE

Exchanging Fear for Faith

Read the passages below, then answer the questions that follow.

NKJV /

For God has not given us a spirit of fear, but of power and of love and of a strong mind.

2 Timothy 1:7

What has God given you?

What is NOT from God?

If fear is not from God, then who or what is causing negative fear in your life?

NIV

Surely God is my salvation; I will trust and not be afraid. The LORD, the LORD Himself, is my strength and my defense; He has become my salvation.
Isaiah 12:2

When we put fear aside and trust God, what are some of the outcomes?

OVERCOMING FEAR, BUILDING TRUST

When we surrender our lives to God and trust Him to heal us, fear dissolves. We are protected, we are healed, and we are safe. We take a step out of the box of hurt and shame and we realize life has been waiting. The sun is shining, the birds are singing, and life has new meaning. You are freed by the simple act of surrender and trust. There will be days you will want to go back into the "safety" of your box – DON'T do it! God has a plan, He is making a way, and He is working all things for GOOD for those who love Him (Romans 8:28). When we choose to trust, we gain confidence and security. Trust comes in and heals what has been damaged. Our name changes from "Hurting" to "OVERCOMER."

He tells us, step by step, what to do to trust in Him, and He reveals the outcome if we do. God is asking you to trust Him with ALL your heart and to keep nothing from Him. Don't lean on what you know. Your grid has been broken and you are not seeing clearly. Acknowledge Him in EVERYTHING you do, say, think, and believe. When you have applied these three directives, the outcome is a straight path right into the arms of the One who loves you so much that He gave His life for you. Trust is essential; it is the key to surrender and the agent for true healing.

SURELY GOD IS MY SALVATION; I WILL
TRUST AND NOT BE AFRAID. THE LORD, THE
LORD HIMSELF, IS MY STRENGTH AND MY
DEFENSE; HE HAS BECOME MY SALVATION.

ISAIAH 12:2

EXERCISE
Trusting God

Read the passage below and answer the following questions.

NASB

Trust in the Lord with all your heart, and
do not lean on your own understanding,
in all your ways acknowledge Him and
He WILL make your paths straight.
Proverbs 3:5-6, emphasis added

What are the three directives God gives us?

What is the promise for following them?

EXERCISE
Releasing Control

Find a quiet place. You can either kneel or lay flat on your back. I want you to focus on your hands. Close them with a tight fist and then slowly release them. Do this a couple of times. Notice the tension in your hands, body, and even your mind when your hands are in a fist. When you release and open your hands, notice how your body feels. Is the tension gone? Does your mind feel relaxed? This is the same thing that happens to your mind and body when you try to control your life.

Stay in that position and, with your hands OPEN, pray. Pray for God to take what has been binding you up. Pray for healing and a release of control. Keep your hands open the whole time, ready to release control and then receive all God has for you. You may want to do this exercise several times this week to remind yourself what the feelings of release and trust are like versus the feelings of control and tension. Keep praying! Keep pressing into God and HE WILL MAKE YOUR PATH STRAIGHT!

JOURNAL REFLECTION

Let's start to reset our brain to focus on ALL that truly is right, instead of focusing on all that's wrong. Write all the times God has been faithful. Write how many times you have seen answered prayers. Write what you are thankful about in your life, and write what you are thankful about in yourself. I encourage you to start or end your journal writing with this everyday. This may be hard at first, but start small. Think of the little things around you or even the little things you like about yourself. I encourage you to write at least three things you are grateful for each day for the next week! WHAT? I know, but YOU CAN DO IT! In order to trust, we need to look back on all God has done, the ways He has provided, and embrace the good in who He has made us to be. So, NO EXCUSES, just write.

WEEKLY BIG 3

01 **What is God asking you to release to Him this week? What will you receive in exchange?**

What "aha!" moments or chapter highlights stood out to you this week? *02*

03 **What three next steps can you take as you continue making exchanges with God?**

07. FORGIVENESS

"IF WE CONFESS OUR SINS, HE IS FAITHFUL
AND JUST AND WILL FORGIVE US OUR SINS AND
PURIFY US FROM ALL UNRIGHTEOUSNESS."
1 JOHN 1:9

VIDEO NOTES

07. FORGIVENESS

I could write so much about forgiveness. It has been the final piece in the puzzle of my healing and freedom, and I know it can be yours.

When I discuss forgiveness with people, I often hear questions like, "Why should I forgive when I haven't done anything wrong?" or "How can I forgive when I'm the one who has done the damage?" People also tell me that they can't forgive the person who has wronged them, or that they will never forgive themselves. It breaks my heart to see these people rot inside because of the wrongdoings of another person, or beat themselves up for theirs. For many, it is as if it happened yesterday, even years after whatever transgression has taken place. They relive the nightmare over and over.

The effects of these wrongful acts spill over to every area of their life. Their relationships suffer, their body suffers, and they spiritually suffer. These painful situations leave them jaded, guarded, untrusting of others, and, for some of them, bitter and shut off. And yet, there is still a deep desire to be free from this heaviness. Perhaps you also have been feeling this way, and perhaps you have some questions about it. "How can I stop this cycle?" "When will it end?" "What is the key to truly being healed from all this pain?"

Let's explore those questions together.

FORGIVING MY MOM

As you've heard and read, my mom's life and my relationship with her were rife with pain and struggle. Growing up, I longed for a mommy who would be able to love me the way other moms seemed to love their kids. I know my mom loved me in her way, but I was not the main focus in her life. I felt abandoned and alone, wishing she would get the help she needed to care for me.

Years went by, and my mom, who was plagued by her own demons, became almost nonexistent in my life. I missed what I dreamed of having, and the reality of what I did have left me angry, hurt, and jaded. I committed myself to trusting God, going to therapy, and then began the arduous task of trying to make sense of all I had done and all that had been done to me. I fought hard and was determined to get better. After two years of therapy, my life and actions started to make sense and I could feel my heart and mind healing. It felt so good to feel freedom and to feel loved by God in a way I never thought I would.

However, there still was this underlying pain that seemed to be there — no matter how hard I tried to heal. What more could I do? I thought I had left no stone unturned. God was Lord of my life and I was walking in a worthy manner. WHY WAS I STILL HURTING?! Then the Lord spoke one word to me that changed my life forever: "FORGIVE."

To begin this process, I started to think about my mom's childhood, her anguish growing up, and how she had a story of pain, too. It didn't excuse her from what she had done, but it made me see her with empathy rather than hurt.

What happened next was the missing piece I had been searching for. The power of the pain she had caused disappeared. My past pain, her lack of love, and all my own bad choices just faded. Forgiveness softened the last part of my hard heart. Forgiveness took away the power this trauma held over my life. It was like a light was turned on and the darkness disappeared.

I wish I could say that my forgiveness changed my mom. Sadly, it didn't. But, it did change me! I was free to move forward with my life, without constantly reliving the pain of my past in everything I did. Forgiveness was for me, and it indeed has set me free. Forgiving my mom helped me to see how much God loves me and forgives me daily. He died so I could be forgiven of all my wrongdoings. His forgiveness is why I am free!

EXERCISE
Identifying the Need to Forgive

Spend some time answering the questions below. If you get stuck, ask God to help reveal the answers.

What emotion or words come to mind when you think of forgiveness?

Is it easier to forgive yourself or others?

Who in your life do you need to forgive? (This may be yourself.)

What burden(s) would be lifted if you were able to forgive those who hurt you?

God loves you; He has forgiven you of ALL your sins.

FORGIVENESS FROM GOD

Do you believe God is a God of forgiveness? To really know the heart of Jesus, we must listen when He speaks. Throughout the scriptures, He taught to forgive others and, in turn, you will be forgiven. There is no greater moment this is shown than when Jesus is on the cross.

When I think about this act, I'm reminded of the great sacrifice it took for Him to come down from Heaven to walk the earth, leaving His throne and His Father, only to die a gruesome death. What love He has for us! This part of the story breaks me every time I read it. There He was, beaten beyond recognition, with people mocking and spitting on Him. He could have called angels in that very moment to strike down His oppressors. With one thought, He could have commanded the ground and it would have devoured those inflicting this pain. Instead, Jesus displayed the very deepest part of His heart. He cried out to His Father, "Forgive them, for they know not what they do!" (Luke 23:34).

Even as He was dying, His heart cried out for forgiveness for His people. God loves you; He has forgiven you of ALL your sins – past, present, and future. This forgiveness ensures our freedom.

EXERCISE

God's Heart of Forgiveness

Let's read more about the heart of God and how He feels about forgiveness. Read the Scriptures below and answer the accompanying questions.

NIV

Blessed is the one whose transgressions are forgiven, whose sins are covered. Blessed is the one whose sin the Lord does not count against them and in whose spirit is no deceit. **Psalm 32:1-2**

What is God saying about what He does when He forgives one of His own?

NIV

If we confess our sins, He is faithful and just and will forgive us our sins and purify us from all unrighteousness.
1 John 1:9

What is the result of His forgiveness?

NIV /

For I will forgive their wickedness
and will remember their sins no more.
Hebrews 8:12

When Jesus forgives, He forgives unlike any human can.
What does He say He does after He forgives you?

WHAT THE BIBLE REVEALS ABOUT FORGIVENESS

By reading the Bible, we see clearly that God wants us to forgive others so we can be free from the power they hold in our life. Forgiveness is not an act of emotion, but rather an act of will. You have to choose to forgive, whether you feel like it or not. Holding on to pain produces bitterness and will cause you to remain in bondage to whatever has happened to you. There is NO freedom in this.

Let's spend some time breaking down a passage that I believe reveals what forgiveness looks like and the reasons it is so important. As you read, make note of what stands out to you.

NASB /

Let all bitterness and wrath and anger and clamor and slander be put away from you, along with all malice. Be kind to one another, tenderhearted, forgiving each other, just as God in Christ also has forgiven you. **Ephesians 4:31-32**

The first thing I'd like to focus on in this passage is the word "bitterness." It is a very powerful word, and the Bible shows how destructive it can be. Bitterness unchecked leads to so many ailments we have today, like depression, anxiety, rage, and addiction. The Bible says bitterness will rot us to the core of our beings, stripping us of an abundant life (Proverbs 14:13). This is why it is so important to allow God to remove this bitterness from your heart.

Now, reread this line: "Let all bitterness and wrath and anger and clamor and slander be put away from you, along with all malice." Notice the "...be put away..." part. This is not something you can do; you need to have someone take it from you. God wants to come in and take all this junk away, but you have to let Him.

You may be wondering how God removes pain in our hearts. Supernaturally, yes, but He also gives us some action steps to remove this bitterness, anger, and wrath from our lives. If you want to be free from the burdens you carry, then you need to forgive, be kind, and be tenderhearted. This means there are some action steps that you must take.

EXERCISE
Steps to Forgiveness

What in your life needs to be "put away?"

How would you benefit from this being removed?

What three action steps do you find in this verse to help remove your pain? Explain what each of those will look like in your life today.

Without utilizing these three steps, you always will carry the guilt of your past and the shame will continue into your future. I can't reiterate this enough: FORGIVENESS is key. Let it go! Take back the power and let the Creator of the Universe – not the pain of your past – control your life!

ACCEPTING FORGIVENESS

Forgiving Myself

As you've heard, my past has not been the greatest example of holy living. In fact, it has been a "WHAT NOT TO DO" guide if you want to live a happy and fulfilled life. When I was married to my previous husband, I had so much unresolved anger that I lived with daily. Together, we went into ministry believing that all of our problems would vanish if we could just ignore our hurts and serve. Well, as you can imagine, this is not how it played out. Hiding our pain made things worse. I became angry and distant, and the hurt became more than I could bear. I remember thinking that I just wanted out; I wanted to leave everything – the ministry and my marriage.

At that time, my mom had finally left my dad and everyone knew our once-hidden secrets. We were a broken family. Camelot fell. The truth that we were not the perfect family we tried to portray for so long was revealed. When this happened, it was like the floodgates of all the emotions I had been holding in for years busted open, and it threw me into a complete mental breakdown. I could not cope with life, ministry, or my marriage. I felt so alone. My husband (at the time) did the best he could to minister to me, but I was completely shut down. I wanted out of it all.

When you live in bitterness and unresolved hurt for a long time, you start to have thoughts you never thought you would, and you start doing things you never would have even considered before. I was searching for anything to make me happy, to numb the pain, or to escape my reality. Unfortunately, I thought an illicit relationship was my answer. I felt so swept up in my pain, so I justified every thought I was having. In fact, I actually thought this would make me happy. I was wrong. This relationship compounded the pain. The hurt it caused my now ex-husband and the continued shame it brought upon me and my family was more than I could take. "What have I done?" "Who have I become?" "This is it," I thought. "I truly have gone too far." According to the world, I had. I had done the unthinkable, and I lost everything. To me, my identity was "disqualified".

My marriage ended, my ministry was gone, and the relationship I was sure was going to bring escape and fulfillment was over. I was left with just me. I hated it and I hated me. I had hurt so many people I loved, the ministry I cared about was over (rightfully so), and all the people who were affected by this ministry were wounded. What a mess I created. I saw no way out. Hope was gone and I was left with so many inner voices telling me the world would be better without me. It's hard to put into words the shame I felt, because it was so intense that I could barely breathe. Panic attacks were an everyday occurrence and the thought of ending it all was where my mind went all the time. I fully believed that God never would forgive me, and thought I never would be able to forgive myself.

During one exceptionally dark moment, the thoughts that had been reeling through my head for months took their toll. I decided everyone would be better off without me and I would never be able to regain meaning in my life. I tried taking a drive, but that didn't help. I soon found myself at a stop sign.

I saw a bus coming and decided this was the answer to all my problems and everyone else's. I would wait for the oncoming bus to end all this pain. God had a different plan, though. So, He stepped in.

Though it wasn't in a burning bush or something super cool like that, it was miraculous to me. I heard a voice say loud and clear, "Karrie, I love you! I have seen all that you have done and I love you! Not only do I love you, but I have a plan for you." I heard Him speak to my heart, telling me that I was defined by His name, not by my past. Before this moment, I was feeling abandoned, ashamed, confused, and utterly hopeless. As I sat there for what seemed like hours, something happened in my heart. I chose to hold on to the small hope I had that Jesus really meant that we are forgiven and redeemed through Him. I turned my car around and started therapy the next week.

ESV

By this we shall know that we are of the truth and reassure our heart before Him; for whenever our heart condemns us, God is greater than our heart, and He knows everything. **1 John 3:19-20**

God knows it all. When we condemn ourselves, He reassures our heart of who we really are. When we don't start the process of forgiving ourselves and laying EVERYTHING we have down before Him, we lessen the power of the cross. He died so you can be forgiven PERIOD! There is no exception to it; you can't earn it or taint it by your actions. It just is.

JOURNAL REFLECTION

During this time of reflection, ask the Lord to reveal who has caused you pain. Understand that you may have caused your own pain. Then, ask God to take away the burden of your pain. Ask Him to FREE you from the bondage of your past. Then, choose to let it go. Write this down, making a written declaration of your choice to release the power this pain has had over you. You may not feel ready to actually move on – and that's ok – but, acknowledging your need to forgive will start the process of God preparing your heart to actually forgive.

Forgiveness changes bitter people

into better people.

Forgiveness is completely for you. It allows you to be free, for chains to fall, and for you to walk out the rest of your life with hope. When the pain of what has happened comes back up, remind yourself of your commitment to forgive. It's a choice! Choose it regularly and you will see a lightness start to rise up in you. You will love better, you will be more joyful, and your heart will be FREE. Forgiveness changes bitter people into better people. Choose to forgive so you can start to walk in victory.

Answer the following questions as you ask God to remove your pain.

WHAT CONDEMNING THOUGHTS HAVE
YOU HAVE BEEN CARRYING?

HOW DO THESE THOUGHTS HAVE
POWER OVER YOUR LIFE?

WHAT WOULD BE DIFFERENT IF YOU
EXCHANGED THESE THOUGHTS FOR THE
TRUTH OF HOW GOD SEES YOU?

"

*NONE OF US
ARE PERFECT,
AND WE WILL
CONTINUE
TO MAKE
MISTAKES –
THAT IS WHY
JESUS IS SO
CRUCIAL TO
OUR STORY.*

STOP BEATING YOURSELF UP

ESV /

Therefore, if anyone is in Christ, he is a new creation. The old has passed away; behold, the new has come.
2 Corinthians 5:17

Here's the deal: this world needs you. You are no good sitting in a corner beating yourself up for all the stuff you've done wrong. None of us are perfect, and we will continue to make mistakes – that is why Jesus is so crucial to our story. Without Him, we are lost sheep destined for failure and misery with no hope of true redemption. But, when we take hold of God's hand, press into His grace, and release our mistakes before Him, we can start to walk in victory. Don't let your past dictate your future anymore. Rest in the knowledge that you are forgiven and allow that knowledge to penetrate your heart and, in turn, forgive yourself.

Set down the whip you've been using to beat yourself for past sin; it's time to walk in the newness of life. This is freedom. In order to do this, you may need to ask for forgiveness from some people and you may need to have some tough conversations. All of this will lead toward further healing. Don't be afraid to get better and don't be afraid of what people will think. God is not afraid of your scandal! He loves you, He sits with you in your mess, and He is beckoning you to let go of the past and come into His healing grace and let go of the past.

I love what Paul writes in **Philippians 3:13:**

ESV ╱ *"Not that I have already obtained this or am already perfect, but I press on to make it my own, because Christ Jesus has made me His own. Brothers, I do not consider that I have made it my own. But one thing I do: forgetting what lies behind and straining forward to what lies ahead."*

If you didn't know or forgot, it's important to know that Paul was a murderer. He was a truly evil man, but God chose, restored, and used Paul for His glory. Just like Paul, we need to let go of what lies behind and press toward what lies ahead. We need to do this for our healing and for the healing of others. Paul was humbled that God knew his past sins, and was using him anyway. Paul's past never dictated his present or his future. Instead, it kept him always grateful for the GREAT love and forgiveness of his Savior, Jesus Christ!

EXERCISE
Accepting Forgiveness Through God's Grace

Accepting forgiveness and grace truly is about understanding what has been done for you DESPITE you. You have to choose to put the past to rest and move forward into the future God has for you. For me, this journey was longer than expected. By exchanging lies for truth, I eventually allowed God to heal my heart. My past is NOT ME. I can never go back and change what happened, but I can accept God's grace upon my life and free myself from the bondage of my actions.

Read the following verses, then answer the following questions.

ESV /

*Come now, let us reason together, says the LORD: though your sins are like scarlet, they shall be as white as snow; though they are red like crimson, they shall become like wool. **Isaiah 1:18***

What freedom would come to you if you really believed this passage?

ESV/

In Him we have redemption through His blood, the forgiveness of our trespasses, according to the riches of His grace.
Ephesians 1:7

What does Ephesians say that forgiveness is according to?

How are we forgiven?

Grace is the free and unmerited favor of God. The moment you step into Christ's family, you receive grace – not because of you, but because of with Whom you are now identified. It is because of God's grace that He forgives you, and it is because of that same grace that you now can forgive yourself.

How do you feel about the word "grace?"

God makes it clear there are no exceptions; all trespasses are forgiven! If the God of the Universe, perfect in all His ways, says you are forgiven, maybe it's time to believe Him and release the burden of your sin before Him.

JOURNAL REFLECTION

Write a letter of forgiveness. This letter may be to a specific person or it may be written to you. Mention why you are going to forgive them/yourself and be specific about what you are forgiving. Commit this letter to God, keep it, and review it whenever you feel yourself slipping back into your old thoughts.

When Christ was on the cross and said, "Forgive them," what did He say after that? He said, "IT IS FINISHED!" When we choose to forgive and commit it to Christ, we can say with ALL AUTHORITY, "It is finished." By saying this, and really owning it, you take back the power and place it in the most trustworthy place: the hands of your Father. You do not have to show this letter to anyone. But, if you feel you need to make amends with someone, a letter is a great place to start.

WEEKLY BIG 3

01

What is God asking you to release to Him this week? What will you receive in exchange?

What "aha!" moments or chapter highlights stood out to you this week? *02*

03

What three next steps can you take as you continue making exchanges with God?

08. VICTORY

"YET IN ALL THESE THINGS WE ARE
MORE THAN CONQUERORS THROUGH
HIM WHO LOVED US."
ROMANS 8:37

VIDEO NOTES

08. VICTORY

Victory! What a wonderful, wonderful word. Victory literally means "the act of defeating or to win, to know that you have overcome some obstacle or have been freed from a terrible situation!" I love the thought of victory, I love the feeling of victory, and I'm driven for victory in my life and in yours.

CONQUERING MY MOUNTAIN

I was such a competitive kid. I wanted to be the best, and this spilled over into my adulthood. I remember the time I decided to go skiing. I had never gone before and was determined to crush it. I am not the most athletic person, but what I lack in athleticism, I make up for in sheer determination. When the day came, we got all our equipment, paid a small mortgage payment to be able to do this activity, and were off to the slopes. I stood at the bottom of the mountain and saw to my left the "bunny slopes," clearly meant for kids, but in front of me were the ADULT slopes! As I pointed to the mountain in front of me, I asked my friend, "What is that slope?" She told me it was a "double black diamond" and that we would not be going down that today. UMMMM, does she not know me? The mere fact that she told me I could not or would not be doing that today did not sit well with this A-type personality. It was time to learn and show her WHAT'S UP and that I would, IN FACT, be conquering said mountain!

Before we could take on the "double black diamond" mountain, we started with the bunny hill. I was so embarrassed as I careened down next to toddlers who were learning techniques called "pizza" and "french fries." I knew I was learning a valuable lesson, but I was just left feeling humiliated...and hungry. After a small snack (yes, pizza and french fries...seriously how could I not?), I was "ready" for the double black diamond. HAHAHAHA. Can you tell where this is going?

My sweet friend kept insisting this was a bad idea, but what did she know? I mean, she had only been skiing since SHE WAS BORN! We got on the ski lift, (which is a whole other story) and then started going higher and higher. As we ascended into THE HEAVENS, clouds began surrounding us and we could only see about a foot in front of us. In my head, I was thinking, "HMMMMM, maybe my friend was right..." Of course, I kept this thought inside my head so my friend wouldn't know how I was feeling.

So, there we were, standing at the top. I looked over at my friend and realized that she did not seem very confident in any of this. I said, "Let's just take it slow, I'll just 'pizza' all the way down." What a doofus. She went ahead of me, my guess was so she could catch me if I started rolling and created a large snowball with my body. I started slow, you know, feeling the vibes of the mountain. I tried to connect with the mountain by talking to it, saying, "Speak to me mountain. Teach me your ways." My speed started to pick up and I went from 'pizza' to 'FRENCH FRIES!!!' I saw my friend coming up on my right, looking dumbfounded and utterly helpless. As I soared by her, I yelled "NO FEAR!" I was doing it; I was attacking this mountain. I came to win; victory was mine! UNTIL...

You see, unbeknownst to me, there are these little things on the slopes called "moguls." They are little bumps made of snow to "make your ski run more fun." THEY ARE NOT FUN! I was speeding down this hill so fast that I could barely see anything, with snow smacking my goggles. Then, all of the sudden, BOOM, I was airborne! I hit a mogul and went flying for what seemed like an hour. I was tossed high into the air and my life flashed before my eyes. As I landed (not gracefully, I should add), my body hit the ground like a rag doll being tossed out of an animal's mouth. SNOW WAS EVERYWHERE! I just laid there with freezing snow in my mouth, my goggles, and in every open orifice you can imagine.

The mountain won. That day spelled defeat for me. I was beaten up, bruised, and humiliated. I was so stupid to try and attack something so big with such little training. Luckily I was ok, but my ego was not. I walked the rest of the way down the mountain. When my friend came up to me afterward, she screamed out, "THAT WAS AWESOME!" What?! "Awesome" was not the word that came to my mind after that.

She proceeded to say she could not believe how far I made it and was blown away that in the midst of a very dangerous situation that I had no experience in, I was yelling, "NO FEAR!" She told me that it took her years to get up enough courage to do the double black diamond, and she was inspired by my drive to conquer the impossible! This was unexpected praise, and something started to stir in me. Maybe this wasn't total defeat. In fact, maybe the mountain didn't win. Victory for me in that moment was the fact that I went for it. I didn't let my fear dictate my actions.

Reflecting on that experience reminds me that victory isn't always defined by absolute triumph. Victory really is defined by the drive and will to do what you know you are called to do, even if you don't conquer it the first time.

I have gone skiing many times since that day, and although I'm far from being a professional, I can do any black diamond anywhere with confidence.

But, honestly, I am more proud of myself for my first attempt than all the attempts after. I went for it – despite the odds! I chose to believe that I could do something bigger than my skill set. Yes, I was slightly wrong, but I DID IT! It gave me the confidence to keep going. If I made it that far the first time, how much farther will I make it the next time?

WHAT IS THE BLACK DIAMOND IN YOUR LIFE?

WHAT AREA DO YOU NEED TO BEGIN CONQUERING?

As you walk in your hurt
and pain, know that God
is listening.

WHAT IS VICTORY?

Victory isn't as much about the destination as it is about the journey. We often think that we have to be completely free from a situation or feeling in order to have freedom or victory in our lives. This is not true! Victory comes in NOT giving up. Victory comes in understanding that your goal is to love God more, love His people better, and to experience His guidance along the way. This attitude will allow you to ease up on yourself and the expectations of perfection you have. By shifting your focus, you allow freedom and victory to take root deep in your heart. There are no quick fixes (you learn nothing with these), and you might repeat the same patterns that got you into a victim mindset. I know we all want to be free and to have victory right away, but the learning process has power on its own.

As you walk in your hurt and pain and seek victory over it, know that God is listening. He does not want to just heal you for the moment, but He truly wants you to be healed for the long run. If we try to rush "victory," we may not learn all we need to avoid repeating or returning to the victim mentality.

EXERCISE
Joy in Trials

NASB /

> Consider it all joy, my brethren, when
> you encounter various trials, knowing
> that the testing of your faith produces
> endurance. And let endurance have its
> perfect result, so that you may be perfect
> and complete, lacking in nothing.
> **James 1:2-4**

**When reading James, what does he say is the result of the trial
we are facing?**

Why do you think God wants you to consider facing trials as joy?

Yes, God has the power to take all the hurt away, and sometimes He does. But, because He loves you so much, He wants you to learn how to lean on Him more and more. Life is hard and there will always be trials and hurts that we must face, but when we understand that God is our refuge (Psalm 46:1) and that we can depend on Him, He will have given you one of the best tools for victory in your life. Don't rush this process. Take time to work through the steps we have gone over and see if there are any areas that God is prompting you to spend more time on. Allow Jesus to dictate your healing process, timeline, and journey. He knows EXACTLY what is best for you.

JOURNAL REFLECTION

Before you continue, read these questions and reflect on your answers:

In what areas of your life are you praying for victory?

What are some expectations you need to surrender before the Lord in order to free you to let the journey of victory begin?

If victory is more about the journey of freedom, then where are you on that journey?

Victory does not mean that you will never again have problems or even that the hurts you have right now automatically will be gone. One day, we will be with the Lord and there will be no more hurt or pain (Revelation 21:4). I am so excited for this day, but, until then, we live in a fallen world. It will help us to understand that God is with us in the midst of the pain, that because of Him we will have victory, and that His timing for healing is perfect.

EXERCISE
Renewing Strength

 ESV

But they who wait on the LORD shall renew their strength; they shall mount up with wings like eagles, they shall run and not be weary, they shall walk and not faint.
Isaiah 40:31

What must we do first?

What are the benefits?

Which area of your life would benefit most from this? Perhaps it's how you manage your team at work, love your children, serve at church, or perhaps, it's something else.

God desires for you to be an overcomer. He talks about this many times in His Scriptures. In order to soar, to be free, and to have true victory, you MUST wait UPON the Lord. I know I keep repeating this, but it really does come back to surrender. Surrendering your plans, your timing, and your healing before the Lord. The good news is the promise that, when you do wait upon the Lord, He WILL renew you. He will make you soar and you will not be weary anymore.

THREE STEPS ON THE PATH TO VICTORY

Victory shows itself in many ways, probably more than you may have thought. You will know that you are experiencing victory when the guilt and shame of your pain doesn't have power over you anymore. Read that again. There will be a day when whatever it is that has kept you in this victim mentality will not have power over you. Until that day comes, keep applying the truths you have learned. I believe there are some great steps you can take to start down the path to victory.

1. SHARE YOUR STORY.
In the story of the Samaritan woman, isn't it amazing to hear how God met her in her loneliness? Yes, there were moments of painful truth, but this solely was for her freedom. As we see Jesus pour out His love before her, we see hope and power come back to her shamed spirit. As we read the Scripture, we see this woman RUN back to the village to share this good news. She didn't wait to have complete freedom before she shared her story, she didn't wait until she had completed 14 Bible classes, or had joined a small group. No, she went THAT day!

You see, victory isn't about perfection; victory is knowing you are imperfect and that GOD STILL loves you! Part of her healing and her freedom came in her sharing! There is power in sharing. It takes it out of your head and the words you share can then bring healing. When you see that someone else also struggles, and they don't feel alone because of your story, tremendous healing happens for you. All the junk that has happened wasn't in vain because God used it for His glory. This has been such a therapeutic thing for me in my own life.

 NIV

I waited patiently for the LORD; He turned to me and heard my cry. He lifted me out of the slimy pit, out of the mud and mire; He set my feet on a rock and gave me a firm place to stand. He put a new song in my mouth, a hymn of praise to our God. Many will see and fear the LORD and put their trust in Him.
Psalm 40:1-3

After we cry out to the Lord and He delivers us, He puts a NEW song in our mouth. But that's not all that happens. Psalm 40 says, "MANY will see and fear the Lord and put their TRUST in Him" because of YOU and your story. I added that last part, because that is what He means! Your story matters. Don't be mistaken; you don't have to wait until you're totally free to share your story. Sharing your story will start to bring healing to your soul. You will begin to see that you are not alone, and that your story, and the redemption that God is bringing to it, will change lives. This is powerful. Vulnerability brings healing, and if you want to start down the path to healing, sharing your story with someone is the start.

A great place to start sharing is with a trusted friend. I know it's scary, but you will see it's less scary once you do it! You can also start by sharing a small portion of your story with your small group. There are many places you can share and it does not have to be a big platform or in front of a lot of people. Sitting on a couch with a hurting friend and sharing what God is doing and has done in your life will bring powerful healing to your heart and hope to your friend. Pray that God gives you the opportunity to share how He has been working. It will heal you in more ways than I can write!

JOURNAL REFLECTION

Write your story — beginning, middle, and end.

EXERCISE
Sharing Your Story

Where will you start to share your story? Not sharing is not an option; it truly will be a place for healing. (This can even be with a counselor - that counts!)

How will sharing your story benefit you?

* We'd love to hear your story! Email us at mystory@wearefreedommovement.org.

2. SERVE IN YOUR GIFTING

Serving is a great way to get perspective on your own life. When you see women who are suffering or a child who is hurt and you are able to help in some way, all of a sudden the focus is off you. You begin to realize that everyone has a story, we are all in need of healing, and your perspective starts to become God's perspective. We need each other and we need to be used. When we're used in this way, we feel valued and that brings great healing. You have gifts that God has given you. No one was created without something to offer, whether it's speaking, singing, painting, baking, or even listening. All are gifts that are needed to bring healing to others. I have a few gifts, but I am lacking in many areas (just ask my husband).

When God called me to start Freedom Movement, I knew He was going to have to surround me with many women with very strong gifts. For example, I am terrible at organization and attention to details. NOT. MY. THING! I knew in order to run a loving, effective organization, we would need someone who could rein me in and take care of the details. I prayed hard for this person. SHE CAME! I have seen thousands of women's lives radically changed because of God's hands on Freedom Movement, but none of this could have happened without organization. If the women on my team thought that their gifting was "less than" because it didn't include some kind of "BIG offering" or "platform," our organization would fail. I am keenly aware that I would not be doing what I am without others around me using their unique gifts. This world needs you. It needs what you can offer.

In Matthew 10, Jesus talks to His disciples about going into cities and preaching God's Word. He gives the directives of what to do and what not to do. He gives warning and also encouragement to this great task, but He concludes this passage with a tangible step.

MSG/

...This is a large work I've called you into, but don't be overwhelmed by it. It's best to start small. Give a cool cup of water to someone who is thirsty, for instance. The smallest act of giving or receiving makes you a true apprentice. You won't lose out on a thing.
Matthew 10:42

"Don't get overwhelmed," He says. Start small. Do you bake? Bake for a family in need or take a meal to someone hurting. Your church needs you. YES, YOU! Can you smile? Get involved with greeting at your church. Some people have not been smiled at all week and just saying "hi" can bring healing to someone that is hurting. Serve at a women's shelter or at church.

Whatever you do, JUST SERVE SOMEWHERE. The world needs your unique perspective and you need theirs, too. Getting out of your story for a little bit will help you to really see the world from a broader perspective. So, think about it. Find your gifts!

EXERCISE
Recognizing Your Gifts

What are a few things you are good at? (Don't know? What do people say you're good at?)

Where is a small area you can start sharing your gifts? (Taking a spiritual gifts test is very helpful and finding what your gifts are can help you figure out where you would be a good fit for helping out.)

Stop right now. Ask God to start revealing where you can serve. Write this down.

3. CHOOSE JOY

I know this sounds cliché, but choosing joy no matter your situation will help you walk towards victory. Victory does not always mean life is perfect, but victory is a state of mind. When you choose to be joyful, you are choosing to be GRATEFUL, which in turn can produce victory over some of the toughest situations.

NASB /
...Do not be grieved, the JOY of the Lord is your STRENGTH! ***Nehemiah 8:10***

Joy does not mean that you will be "happy" all the time or that nothing will affect you. Joy is deep within you. It sustains you through the hardest of times. It gives peace in the midst of deep pain. Joy is a choice that we must choose daily. Allowing the joy of the Lord to fill your heart gives you peace in the toughest situations. This peace goes beyond what we can understand because it is supernatural. When my mom died, I was so very sad, but I cried out to God and He comforted me. I received a peace from Him that defied understanding.

ESV/

And the peace of God, which surpasses all understanding, will guard your hearts and your minds in Christ Jesus.
Philippians 4:7

What is the outcome of this peace that God gives? I like to think about it like this: choosing joy produces gratitude, which then gives peace in any situation. Joy and gratitude are what we choose to focus on, and the outcome of that is peace. Peace comes to you from God, and it is the very thing that will guard your heart and mind. By taking the step to CHOOSE joy and allow gratitude to be at the forefront of your mind, peace will supernaturally enter in, and where there is peace, there is VICTORY!

God is at work. His desire is for you to be complete, lacking NOTHING. So, choose joy knowing that God will be faithful to see you through anything life may throw your way. A great way to help continue choosing joy is to keep up the gratitude journal we started in week six. This will help you begin or end your day reflecting on the blessings in your life.

REFLECTING ON YOUR JOURNEY

Let's take a few moments to recap the areas we have discussed. Pray over each one and ask God to show you if there is any area in which you need to stop and spend some more time. Remember, this is a JOURNEY. Healing and freedom take some time, but when you are committed to moving forward and you surrender your hurts before the Lord, victory WILL come!

LOVE

Remember that God loves you so much that He died for you. Nothing you have done or ever will do can separate you from His love. When we are loved purely, we can rise above whatever keeps us stuck, knowing that THE LIVING GOD who calls us HIS own gives us our identity.

IDENTITY

It is time to stop placing our identity in the mistakes that we have made or things that have been done to us. Instead, we must re-label ourselves with who God says we are: we are HIS CHILDREN and heirs to HIS THRONE. He has made us to be overcomers because of His great sacrifice. Begin the task of giving yourself new names, new labels, and walk with confidence because of WHO YOU ARE, not what you have done!

CONFESSION AND SURRENDER

Acknowledging the burdens you are carrying before the Lord and getting honest about what really is going on allows you to turn from your past and move toward a healed future. Remember that you are already forgiven, but the act of confession allows for repentance so you will move in a new direction. When we confess before the Lord, it allows what we have known in our heads to go deep into our hearts. This will begin the process of surrender, which is letting go of the things you have no control over. Control is what produces anxiety. When we try to control things we have no control over, it messes with our head. The safest you ever will be is when you surrender your hurts, your desires, and your heart over to the Lord. He loves you and only wants what's best for you. Choosing to surrender is the key to freedom.

GRIEVING

We discussed healthy and unhealthy ways to grieve. Grieving is meant for you to acknowledge a hurt and move you through that pain into healing. Getting stuck on one aspect of grieving has the ability to stifle your life and keep you from being free. When grieving is done properly and through the grid of God's Word, it can be an essential tool to move past a hurt or offense and into victory over it. Learning to grieve will be useful for the rest of your life, so I encourage you to harness the power that comes when you grieve in a healthy way.

SOUL CARE

Taking time for yourself is not a luxury, it's a necessity! You cannot serve from an empty vessel. Taking care of yourself gives you the ability to be your best self and, in turn, helps you love more freely and serve from a full heart. You are worth the time. God is often calling us from our busy to-do lists and saying, "Come away with Me, daughter; I have much to share with you." It is in these quiet places of soul care that we find ourselves.

TRUST

When we put our trust in God, fear begins to diminish. He longs to show you how trustworthy He is. Trusting God will produce freedom in every area of your life. It is time to step out of your box, trust God with all of your heart, and to allow Him to heal what has been broken. This takes an act of surrender – hand over what you think is best and allow God to show you what is right for your life. Trust takes practice. Learning to trust God will take time. Don't miss an opportunity to put your trust in Him. You will never be disappointed when you fully trust God.

FORGIVENESS

When we forgive, we allow bitterness and anger to leave our lives. Forgiveness frees us to love well, to heal from the past, and it brings light to the darkest parts of our heart. When we forgive, we move the power from the treacherous acts that have been committed to the loving hands of God. Freedom comes when we release our guilt and shame and walk out the rest of our lives with a tender, whole heart. Having healthy boundaries will ensure that your heart is protected and will allow you to have empathy and love without someone taking advantage of you. Pray that God shows you the necessary boundaries in your life that will allow you to forgive and love from a safe place.

VICTORY

How do we know when we are victorious? I will sum it up in one sentence: when the weight of guilt and shame has been removed, you are free. God wants you to be identified by the things above, not by the mistakes you have made or the things that have been done to you. When you realize He takes your mess and makes miracles from it, then you will live life as an overcomer. Ask God to reveal where He wants you to use the gifts He has given you. Not only does this help in the healing process, but it also allows you to have continued victory as you help others feel God's love through the gifts that you bring.

JOURNAL REFLECTION

What are a few things that are sitting heaviest with you that you want to explore more? What will you do to make this happen?

WEEKLY BIG 3

01 What is God asking you to release to Him this week? What will you receive in exchange?

02 What "aha!" moments or chapter highlights stood out to you this week?

03 What three next steps can you take as you continue making exchanges with God?

YOUR JOURNEY IS JUST BEGINNING

As you prepare to close this workbook, I want you to reflect on the journey you have taken over the past several weeks. You have allowed yourself to show up, to invest in yourself, to hear from the Lord, and to be changed. This was no easy task! You had to dig deep to encounter things either about yourself or others that were probably painful to face. Yet, you did it! You should be proud of yourself. It takes a courageous soul to want to "go there." Freedom does not come by just wishing it would happen, you have to do the hard work. And, sweet friend, you did!

Remember that this is a *working* workbook; your journey has just begun. The great thing about having this experience under your belt and this workbook in hand is that you now have tools. You WILL have to deal with grief, forgiveness, and even your trust issues again, and you will find yourself struggling with your identity and questioning the love of God again. BUT NOW, you have tools to use that will direct you to the Word of God and that WILL bring continued healing.

This program is a culmination of 10 years of work for me. It has taken many years to figure out how God led me to victory in many areas of my life and how I continue to see what I need to apply in my life today. I encourage you to not just close this workbook and never look at it again. If you're hurting, stuck, or feeling the pressure of life, open it up, find a Scripture and a truth, and let it sink deep into your spirit. You are a beautiful work in progress! You are a woman who will never go back to who you were and will press forward toward the promised freedom God has for you.

Pray that God continues to reveal things in your life that could keep you stuck, and then pray that He gives you strength to avoid those things. When the TRUTH sets you free, you are free indeed. Pursue God's Truth, even when it feels counterintuitive, and TRUST that you are in the safest hands; the hands of your loving Father who wants to LAVISH good things upon you.

Lastly, always remember this:

 NASB

GREATER is HE who is in you than he who is in the world.
1 John 4:4, Emphasis Added

WHEN THE TRUTH SETS YOU FREE, YOU ARE FREE INDEED!

EXERCISE:
Course Reflection

If you're working through The Exchange as a small group, share your answers with the group.

What was the biggest exchange God has asked you to make in this course?

What "aha!" moments or chapter highlights stood out from this course?

99

*YOU ARE A
BEAUTIFUL WORK IN
PROGRESS! YOU ARE
A WOMAN WHO WILL
NEVER GO BACK TO
WHO YOU WERE
AND WILL PRESS
FORWARD TOWARD
THE PROMISED
FREEDOM THAT GOD
HAS FOR YOU.*

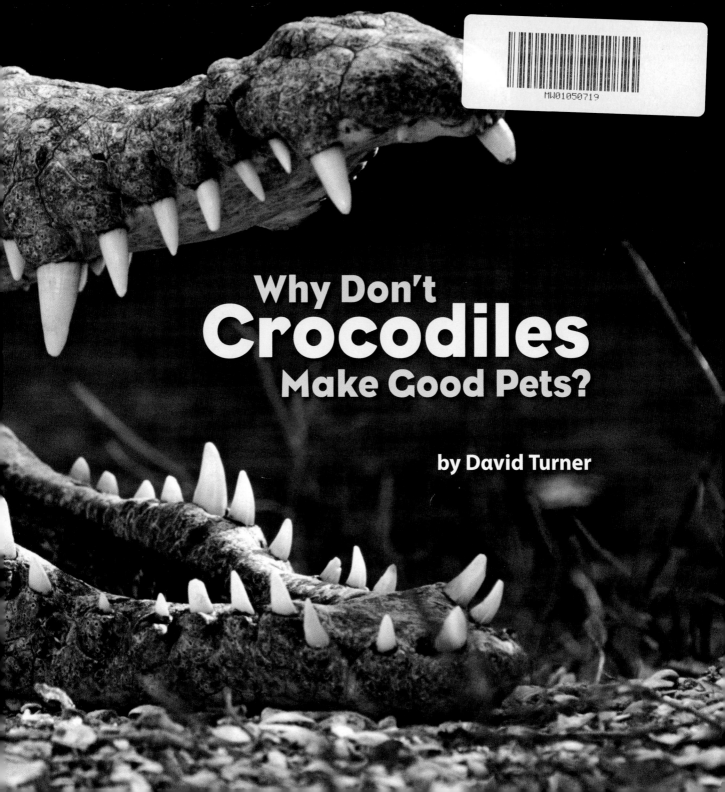

Why Don't Crocodiles Make Good Pets?

by David Turner

MW01050719

Baby animals are cute.

Even baby crocodiles!

But is one cute enough to hold in the palm of your hand?

Not for long!

You might be able to hold a baby crocodile, or hatchling, in the palm of your hand at first. But an adult crocodile would grow to be too big.

Would it be difficult for an adult crocodile
to find something to eat?

Not at all.

A grown-up crocodile eats just about anything.

So why don't crocodiles make good pets?

Because they're crocodiles!

11

From Egg to Adult

- A crocodile hatches from an egg.

- A baby crocodile can stay in its nest for eight weeks.

- A crocodile's life cycle can last as long as 70 years.